QUILTS to warm today's HOME

LEISURE ARTS, INC.
Little Rock, Arkansas

EDITORIAL STAFF
Vice President of Editorial: Susan White Sullivan
Special Projects Director: Susan Frantz Wiles
Director of E-Commerce: Mark Hawkins
Art Publications Director: Rhonda Shelby
Technical Writer: Lisa Lancaster
Technical Associate: Frances Huddleston
Editorial Writer: Susan McManus Johnson
Art Category Manager: Lora Puls
Graphic Artist: Stacy Owens
Imaging Technician: Stephanie Johnson
Prepress Technician: Janie Marie Wright
Photography Manager: Katherine Laughlin
Contributing Photographer: Ken West
Contributing Photo Stylist: Sondra Daniel
Manager of E-Commerce: Robert Young

BUSINESS STAFF
President and Chief Executive Officer: Rick Barton
Vice President of Sales: Mike Behar
Vice President of Finance: Laticia Mull Dittrich
Director of Corporate Planning: Anne Martin
National Sales Director: Martha Adams
Creative Services: Chaska Lucas
Information Technology Director: Hermine Linz
Controller: Francis Caple
Vice President of Operations: Jim Dittrich
Retail Customer Service Manager: Stan Raynor
Vice President of Purchasing: Fred F. Pruss

Library of Congress Control Number: 2012930435

ISBN-13: 978-1-60900-966-3

Table of Contents

Quilts to Warm Today's Home

How comforting it is to create a sweep of soothing patchwork in colors that remind you of home! These eleven homestyle quilts by Nancy Rink feature traditional pieced designs, with lively appliquéd leaves and flowers on several. Instructions are included for a variety of appliqué techniques, and we've provided quilting information that will help you decide how to machine-quilt your project. Whether you make bed quilts, wall hangings, or cozy wraps for use on the sofa, your creations will welcome you home for many years to come. Enjoy the sweetness of stitching each one with the fabrics that warm your heart.

MEET NANCY RINK

A few years ago, Nancy Rink's husband Oliver spotted an ad for a national quilt design contest. He told Nancy she should enter a quilt.

Nancy, who had quilted for years from existing patterns, said, "I don't design quilts."

Oliver replied, "But you could."

She decided to give it a try—and designed a quilt that won the contest!

Since then, Nancy has won numerous awards for her designs, while her amazing quilts have appeared in several popular quilting magazines. She also works with Marcus Fabrics as a quilting consultant, designing patterns for their website and testing their new lines to see how they work in quilts.

"Their fabrics are beautiful," Nancy says. "Sometimes I get to make small suggestions, such as adding one more background fabric or another fabric that pulls all the colors together."

When she isn't holding trunk shows or leading workshops, Nancy enjoys spending time with her husband, family, and dog. She also likes to read and enjoys getting together with quilting friends to sew. About six to eight times per year, she and Oliver vend at California quilt shows.

Nancy says, "My grandmother taught me to sew when I was ten or eleven. We would go to the 'yard-goods store' for fabric. When I was grown, we took a quilting class together. Grandma couldn't stand 'cutting up perfectly good fabric and sewing it back together,' but I love it! I made quilts all through the years my children were growing up.

Nancy maintains her quilting blog at NancyRinkDesigns.blogspot.com. She sells a wide variety of quilting supplies, as well as her beautiful patterns, at NancyRinkDesigns.com. She also loves to hear from quilters on her Facebook page.

Finished Quilt Size: 65" x 85" (165 cm x 216 cm)
Finished Block Size: 10" x 10" (25 cm x 25 cm)

YARDAGE REQUIREMENTS

Yardage is based on 43"/44" (109 cm/112 cm) wide fabric with a usable width of 40" (102 cm).

- $5/8$ yd (57 cm) *each* of 3 assorted red print fabrics
- $5/8$ yd (57 cm) *each* of 5 assorted blue print fabrics
- $5/8$ yd (57 cm) of tan print fabric
- $5/8$ yd (57 cm) of brown print fabric
- $7/8$ yd (80 cm) *each* of 4 assorted cream print fabrics
- $7/8$ yd (80 cm) of cream novelty print fabric (Ours features baseball players.)
- $1^3/8$ yds (1.3 m) of red and blue stripe fabric for inner borders and binding
- $5^1/4$ yds (4.8 m) of fabric for backing

You will also need:

- 73" x 93" (185 cm x 236 cm) piece of batting
- 68 sheets of That Patchwork Place® $8^1/2$" x 11" (22 cm x 28 cm) papers for foundation piecing

CUTTING THE PIECES

*Follow **Rotary Cutting**, page 81, to cut fabric. Cut all strips across the selvage-to-selvage width of the fabric. Inner Borders include extra length for "insurance" and will be trimmed after assembling quilt top center. All measurements include $1/4$" seam allowances.*

From red print #1 fabric:

- Cut 1 strip $2^1/2$"w. From this strip, cut 15 **squares (A)** $2^1/2$" x $2^1/2$".
- Cut 3 strips 3"w. From these strips, cut 29 **squares (B)** 3" x 3".

From red print #2 fabric:

- Cut 2 strips $2^1/2$"w. From these strips, cut 24 **squares (A)** $2^1/2$" x $2^1/2$".
- Cut 2 **strips** 2"w for paper pieced diamond block.
- Cut 1 strip $3^1/4$"w. From this strip, cut 5 squares $3^1/4$" x $3^1/4$". Cut each square *once* diagonally to make 10 **triangles (A2)**.

From red print #3 fabric:

- Cut 1 strip $2^1/2$"w. From this strip, cut 15 **squares (A)** $2^1/2$" x $2^1/2$".
- Cut 1 strip 3"w. From this strip, cut 12 **squares (B)** 3" x 3".

Continued on page 8.

From blue print #1 fabric:
- Cut 1 strip $2^1/_2$"w. From this strip, cut 15 **squares (A)** $2^1/_2$" x $2^1/_2$".
- Cut 3 strips 3"w. From these strips, cut 29 **squares (B)** 3" x 3".

From blue print #2 fabric:
- Cut 2 strips $2^1/_2$"w. From these strips, cut 24 **squares (A)** $2^1/_2$" x $2^1/_2$".
- Cut 2 **strips** 2"w for paper pieced diamond block.
- Cut 1 strip $3^1/_4$"w. From this strip, cut 5 squares $3^1/_4$" x $3^1/_4$". Cut each square *once* diagonally to make 10 **triangles (A2)**.

From blue print #3 fabric:
- Cut 1 strip $2^1/_2$"w. From this strip, cut 15 **squares (A)** $2^1/_2$" x $2^1/_2$".
- Cut 1 strip 3"w. From this strip, cut 12 **squares (B)** 3" x 3".
- Cut 2 **strips** 2"w for paper pieced diamond block.
- Cut 1 strip $3^1/_4$"w. From this strip, cut 5 squares $3^1/_4$" x $3^1/_4$". Cut each square *once* diagonally to make 10 **triangles (A2)**.

From blue print #4 fabric:
- Cut 1 strip $2^1/_2$"w. From this strip, cut 15 **squares (A)** $2^1/_2$" x $2^1/_2$".
- Cut 1 strip 3"w. From this strip, cut 12 **squares (B)** 3" x 3".
- Cut 2 **strips** 2"w for paper pieced diamond block.
- Cut 1 strip $3^1/_4$"w. From this strip, cut 5 squares $3^1/_4$" x $3^1/_4$". Cut each square *once* diagonally to make 10 **triangles (A2)**.

From blue print #5 fabric:
- Cut 2 **strips** 2"w for paper pieced diamond block.
- Cut 1 strip $3^1/_4$"w. From this strip, cut 5 squares $3^1/_4$" x $3^1/_4$". Cut each square *once* diagonally to make 10 **triangles (A2)**.

From tan print fabric:
- Cut 2 strips $2^1/_2$"w. From these strips, cut 24 **squares (A)** $2^1/_2$" x $2^1/_2$".
- Cut 2 **strips** 2"w for paper pieced diamond block.
- Cut 1 strip $3^1/_4$"w. From this strip, cut 5 squares $3^1/_4$" x $3^1/_4$". Cut each square *once* diagonally to make 10 **triangles (A2)**.

From brown print fabric:
- Cut 1 strip $2^1/_2$"w. From this strip, cut 15 **squares (A)** $2^1/_2$" x $2^1/_2$".
- Cut 1 strip 3"w. From this strip, cut 12 **squares (B)** 3" x 3".
- Cut 2 **strips** 2"w for paper pieced diamond block.
- Cut 1 strip $3^1/_4$"w. From this strip, cut 5 squares $3^1/_4$" x $3^1/_4$". Cut each square *once* diagonally to make 10 **triangles (A2)**.

From *each* of 3 cream print fabrics:
- Cut 2 strips $2^1/_2$"w. From these strips, cut 24 **squares (A)** $2^1/_2$" x $2^1/_2$".
- Cut 2 strips 3"w. From these strips, cut 24 **squares (B)** 3" x 3".
- Cut 3 **strips** 2"w for paper pieced diamond block.
- Cut 4 **strips** $2^3/_4$"w for paper pieced diamond block.

From cream #4 print fabric:
- Cut 5 strips $2^{1}/_{2}$"w. From these strips, cut 18 **squares (A)** $2^{1}/_{2}$" x $2^{1}/_{2}$" and 18 **rectangles (C)** $2^{1}/_{2}$" x $6^{1}/_{2}$".
- Cut 2 **strips** 2"w for paper pieced diamond block.
- Cut 4 **strips** $2^{3}/_{4}$"w for paper pieced diamond block.

From cream novelty print fabric:
- Cut 5 strips $2^{1}/_{2}$"w. From these strips, cut 18 **squares (A)** $2^{1}/_{2}$" x $2^{1}/_{2}$" and 18 **rectangles (C)** $2^{1}/_{2}$" x $6^{1}/_{2}$".
- Cut 2 **strips** 2"w for paper pieced diamond block.
- Cut 4 **strips** $2^{3}/_{4}$"w for paper pieced diamond block.

From red and blue stripe fabric:
- Cut 2 **strips** 2"w for paper pieced diamond block.
- Cut 7 strips $2^{1}/_{2}$"w. Sew strips together end to end and recut into 2 **top/bottom inner borders** $2^{1}/_{2}$" x $58^{1}/_{2}$" and 2 **side inner borders** $2^{1}/_{2}$" x $74^{1}/_{2}$".
- Cut 9 **binding strips** $2^{1}/_{4}$"w.

From remaining assorted color print fabrics:
- Cut 132 **rectangles (D)** $2^{1}/_{2}$" x $5^{1}/_{2}$".
- Cut 4 **squares (E)** $3^{1}/_{2}$" x $3^{1}/_{2}$".
- Cut 4 **rectangles (F)** $2^{1}/_{2}$" x $3^{1}/_{2}$".

ASSEMBLING THE BLOCKS

These blocks should be very scrappy. Feel free to randomly mix and match the various strips and triangles. The cutting instructions included extra pieces to allow for freedom in the fabric placement.

Diamond Blocks
1. Photocopy $^{1}/_{4}$ Diamond Block pattern, page 13, onto foundation piecing paper. Make 68 photocopies.
2. Choose 17 red print #1 and 17 blue print #1 **squares (B)**. Cut each square *once* diagonally to make 34 red **triangles** and 34 blue **triangles** for position A5.
3. Referring to pattern for fabric placement and trimming strips as needed, refer to **Foundation Paper Piecing**, page 83, to stitch and flip strips and triangles in numerical order beginning in the A1 position.
4. Sew 4 of the paper pieced $^{1}/_{4}$ Diamond Blocks together to make a **Diamond Block**, making sure A5 triangles are placed in the center. Press seam allowances open. Make 17 Diamond Blocks.

Diamond Block (make 17)

Star Blocks

*Follow **Machine Piecing**, page 82, and **Pressing**, page 83. Use a ¹/₄" seam allowance for piecing.*

1. Choose 4 **squares** (A) and 4 **squares** (B) from 1 cream print, 5 **squares** (A) and 4 **squares** (B) from 1 red print, 4 **squares** (A) from 1 blue print, and 2 **squares** (A) and 2 **rectangles** (C) from cream novelty print.

2. Sew 2 cream novelty print squares (A), and 1 red print square (A) together to make **Unit 1**. Press seam allowances toward red print square.

3. Draw a diagonal line on the wrong side of 4 red print squares (A). Matching right sides, place red print squares on ends of 2 cream novelty print rectangles (C) as shown in **Fig. 1**.

4. Sew each square along drawn lines. Trim ¹/₄" from drawn line as shown in **Fig. 2** and press open to make 2 **Unit 2's**.

5. Draw a diagonal line on the wrong side of 1 cream print square (B). Matching right sides, place cream print square (B) on top of 1 red print square (B). Stitch ¹/₄" from each side of drawn line (**Fig. 3**). Cut along drawn line; press open, pressing seam allowances toward the red print fabric to make 2 **Unit 3's**. Make 8 Unit 3's. Trim each Unit 3 to 2¹/₂" x 2¹/₂".

6. Referring to **Star Block Diagram**, sew 1 Unit 1, 2 Unit 2's, 8 Unit 3's, 4 cream print squares (A), and 4 blue print squares (A) together to make **Star Block**. Repeat Steps 1-6 to make a total of 3 Star Blocks in this color way.

7. Refer to **Additional Star Block Diagrams** and repeat Steps 2-6 to make 3 Star Blocks of each color way to make a total of 18 Star Blocks.

Unit 1

Fig. 1

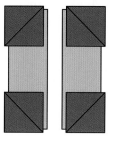

Fig. 2

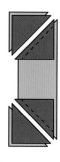

Unit 2

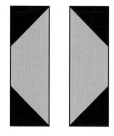

Fig. 3

Unit 3 (make 8)

ASSEMBLING THE QUILT TOP CENTER

*Refer to **Quilt Top Diagram**, page 12, for assembly.*

1. Beginning with a Star Block and alternating blocks, sew 3 Star Blocks and 2 Diamond Blocks together to make **Row 1**. Make 4 Row 1's.
2. Beginning with a Diamond Block and alternating blocks, sew 3 Diamond Blocks and 2 Star Blocks together to make **Row 2**. Make 3 Row 2's.
3. Sew Rows 1 and 2 together to make Quilt Top Center.

ADDING THE BORDERS

1. Refer to **Adding Squared Borders**, page 88, to add **side**, then **top** and **bottom inner borders** to quilt top center.
2. Sew 1 **rectangle (D)**, 1 **square (E)**, and 1 **rectangle (F)** together to make **Border Corner**. Make 4 Border Corners.
3. Randomly sew together 37 **rectangles (D)** to make **Side Outer Border**. Make 2 Side Outer Borders.
4. Sew 1 Side Outer Border to each side of quilt top. It may be necessary to make border seams wider or narrower to adjust the length to fit the quilt top.
5. Randomly sew together 27 rectangles (D) to make **Top Outer Border**. Repeat to make **Bottom Outer Border**.
6. Noting orientation of Border Corners, sew 1 to each end of Top and Bottom Outer Borders. Sew Top and Bottom Outer Borders to quilt top. Again, it may be necessary to make border seams wider or narrower to adjust the length to fit the quilt top.

Star Block Diagram
(make 3)

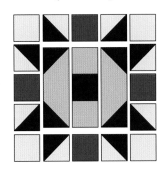

Additional Star Block Diagrams
(make 3 of each color way)

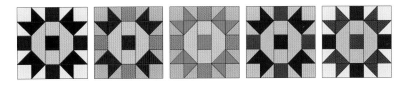

Row 1
(make 4)

Row 2
(make 3)

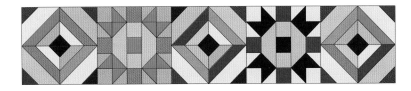

Border Corner (make 4)

FINISHING THE QUILT

Fig. 4

1. Stay-stitch around the outside edge of the quilt top to keep seams from opening during quilting.
2. Follow **Quilting**, page 89, to mark, layer, and quilt. Our quilt is machine quilted with an all-over meandering pattern on the quilt top center, a straight line through the center of the inner border, and wavy lines in each rectangle of the outer border.
3. Sew binding strips together using a diagonal seam (**Fig. 4**) to make a continuous binding strip.
4. Follow **Attaching Binding with Mitered Corners**, page 93, and attach binding.

¹/₄ Diamond Block
(make 68 photocopies)

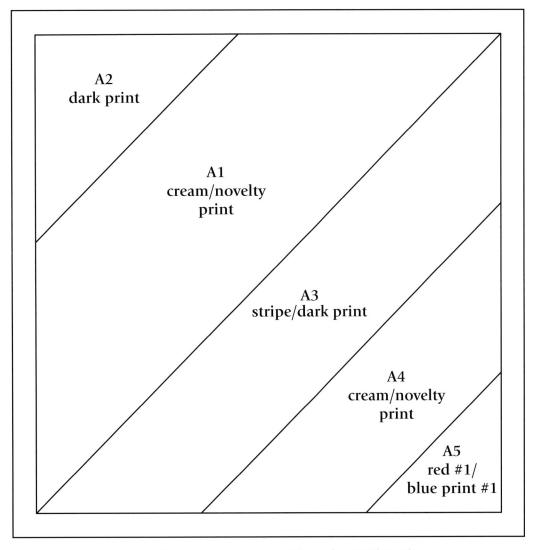

A2
dark print

A1
cream/novelty
print

A3
stripe/dark print

A4
cream/novelty
print

A5
red #1/
blue print #1

EMERALD SPRING

Finished Quilt Size: 84" x 84" (213 cm x 213 cm)
Finished Block Size: 11" x 11" (28 cm x 28 cm)

YARDAGE REQUIREMENTS

*Yardage is based on 43"/44" (109 cm/112 cm) wide
fabric with a usable width of 40" (102 cm).*

- 5^1/$_4$ yds (4.8 m) of white print fabric
- 3^1/$_4$ yds (3 m) of dark green print fabric
- 2^1/$_8$ yds (1.9 m) of medium green print fabric
- 3^3/$_4$ yds (3.4 m) *total* of assorted print fabric in various shades of emerald, mint, lime, and blue green
- ^{3}/$_8$ yd (34 cm) of light green print fabric for piping
- 7^3/$_4$ yds (7.1 m) of fabric for backing

You will also need:

- 92" x 92" (234 cm x 234 cm) piece of batting
- 10 yds (9.1 m) of 1 mm - 5 mm polyester or nylon cord for piping
- No-melt mylar template plastic
- Optional: green machine embroidery thread for Blanket Stitch on leaves and vine
- Optional: Susan Cleveland's Groovin' Piping Trimming Tool (available from piecesbewithyou.com)
- Optional: ^{1}/$_2$" (13 mm) bias pressing bar

CUTTING THE PIECES

*Follow **Rotary Cutting**, page 81, to cut fabric. Cut all
strips across the selvage-to-selvage width of the fabric
unless otherwise indicated. Inner and Outer Borders
include extra length for "insurance" and will be
trimmed after assembling the quilt top center.
All measurements include ^{1}/$_4$" seam allowances.
Use pattern, page 21, and follow **Making and Using
Templates**, page 84, Step 1, to make template for the
leaf pattern.*

From white print fabric:
- Cut 2 **wide strips** 5^1/$_2$"w.
- Cut 2 **medium strips** 3^1/$_2$"w.
- Cut 41 **narrow strips** 1^1/$_2$"w.
- Cut 3 strips 7^1/$_2$"w. From these strips, cut 12 **squares** 7^1/$_2$" x 7^1/$_2$".
- Cut 4 *lengthwise* **middle borders** 9^1/$_2$" x 75^1/$_2$".

From dark green print fabric:
- Cut 10 strips 4^1/$_2$"w. Sew strips together end to end and recut into 4 **outer borders** 4^1/$_2$" x 88".
- Cut 10 **binding strips** 2^1/$_2$"w.
- Cut 7 strips 1^1/$_2$"w. Sew strips together end to end and recut into 2 **side inner borders** 1^1/$_2$" x 59^1/$_2$" and 2 **top/bottom inner borders** 1^1/$_2$" x 61^1/$_2$".
- Refer to **Making A Continuous Bias Strip**, page 92, and use a 28" square to cut **bias strip** for vine 1^1/$_2$" x 425".

From medium green print fabric:
- Cut 4 *lengthwise* **middle borders** 9^1/$_2$" x 75^1/$_2$".

From assorted print fabric in various shades of emerald, mint, lime, and blue green:
- Cut 45 **narrow strips** 1^1/$_2$"w.
- Refer to **Preparing Blanket Stitch or Zigzag Stitch Appliqués**, page 85, and use template to cut 240 leaves.

From light green print fabric for piping:
- Cut 9 **piping strips** 1"w.

TIPS FOR MAKING THE BLOCKS:

To prevent distortion and achieve good results, use the following tips:

- Starch and press fabric pieces.
- Set a short stitch length on your sewing machine to prevent the Units from coming apart after cutting.
- Use an accurate $1/4$" seam allowance.
- Press seam allowances toward the darker strips, being careful not to stretch the strips when pressing.
- When cutting the Strip Sets, place them seam allowance side up. This prevents the Strip Sets from shifting and allows you to be more accurate when cutting.
- Check after every 2-3 cuts to make sure you are still cutting the Units perpendicular to the seams. Square up the end of the Strip Set if necessary before cutting more Units.
- Match seams and pin before joining Units.

ASSEMBLING THE BLOCKS

Follow **Machine Piecing**, *page 82, and* **Pressing**, *page 83. Use a $1/4$" seam allowance for piecing.*

Block A

1. Alternating greens with white, sew 6 assorted green print and 5 white print **narrow strips** together to make **Strip Set A**. Strip Set A should measure $11^1/2$"w including seam allowances. Using a variety of green narrow strips, make 3 Strip Set A's. Cut across Strip Set A's at $1^1/2$" intervals to make **Unit 1**. Make 78 Unit 1's.

2. Repeat Step 1 using 5 assorted green print and 6 white print narrow strips to make **Strip Set B**. Strip Set B should measure $11^1/2$"w including seam allowances. Make 3 Strip Set B's. Cut across Strip Set B's at $1^1/2$" intervals to make **Unit 2**. Make 65 Unit 2's.

3. Alternating Units and using Units cut from different Strips Sets for the scrappiest look, sew 6 Unit 1's and 5 Unit 2's together to make **Block A**. Block A should measure $11^1/2$" x $11^1/2$" including seam allowances. Make 13 Block A's.

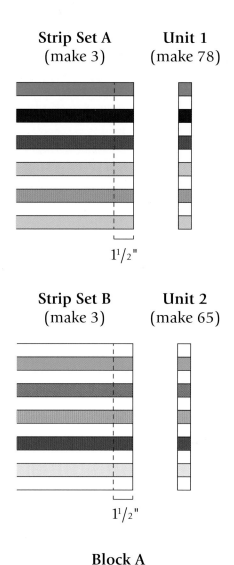

Strip Set A
(make 3)

Unit 1
(make 78)

$1^1/2$"

Strip Set B
(make 3)

Unit 2
(make 65)

$1^1/2$"

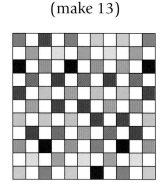

Block A
(make 13)

Block B

1. Sew 2 assorted green print **narrow strips**, 2 white print **narrow strips**, and 1 white print **medium strip** together to make **Strip Set C**. Strip Set C should measure 7$\frac{1}{2}$"w including seam allowances. Using a variety of green narrow strips, make 2 Strip Set C's. Cut across Strip Set C's at 1$\frac{1}{2}$" intervals to make **Unit 3**. Make 48 Unit 3's.

2. Sew 2 assorted green print **narrow strips** and 1 white print **wide strip** together to make **Strip Set D**. Strip Set D should measure 7$\frac{1}{2}$"w including seam allowances. Using a variety of green narrow strips, make 2 Strip Set D's. Cut across Strip Set D's at 1$\frac{1}{2}$" intervals to make **Unit 4**. Make 48 Unit 4's.

3. Sew 1 Unit 3 and 1 Unit 4 together to make **Unit 5**. Make 48 Unit 5's.

4. Sew 1 green print **narrow strip** and 1 white print **narrow strip** together to make **Strip Set E**. Strip Set E should measure 2$\frac{1}{2}$"w including seam allowances. Using a variety of green narrow strips, make 4 Strip Set E's. Cut across Strip Set E's at 1$\frac{1}{2}$" intervals to make **Unit 6**. Make 96 Unit 6's.

5. Sew 2 Unit 6's together to make **Unit 7**. Make 48 Unit 7's.

6. Sew 1 Unit 7 to each end of 1 Unit 5 to make **Unit 8**. Make 24 Unit 8's.

7. Sew 1 Unit 5 to each side of 1 white print **square** to make **Unit 9**. Make 12 Unit 9's.

8. Sew 2 Unit 8's and 1 Unit 9 together to make **Block B**. Block B should measure 11$\frac{1}{2}$" x 11$\frac{1}{2}$" including seam allowances. Make 12 Block B's.

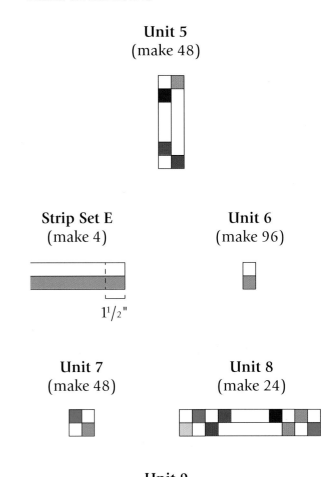

Unit 5
(make 48)

Strip Set E
(make 4)

1$\frac{1}{2}$"

Unit 6
(make 96)

Unit 7
(make 48)

Unit 8
(make 24)

Unit 9
(make 12)

Strip Set C
(make 2)

Unit 3
(make 48)

1$\frac{1}{2}$"

Strip Set D
(make 2)

Unit 4
(make 48)

1$\frac{1}{2}$"

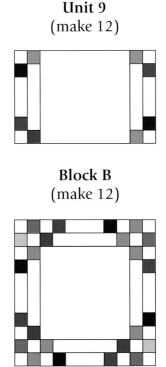

Block B
(make 12)

ASSEMBLING THE QUILT TOP CENTER

Refer to photo, for assembly.

1. Beginning with a Block A and alternating blocks, sew 3 Block A's and 2 Block B's together to make **Row 1**. Make 3 Row 1's.

2. Beginning with a Block B and alternating blocks, sew 3 Block B's and 2 Block A's together to make **Row 2**. Make 2 Row 2's.

3. Sew Row 1's and 2's together to make Quilt Top Center.

4. Refer to **Adding Squared Borders**, page 88, to add **side** then **top** and **bottom inner borders** to quilt top center.

PREPARING THE MIDDLE BORDERS

1. To create a top/bottom border pattern, cut a strip of freezer paper $9^1/_2$" x $75^1/_2$". Referring to **Fig. 1**, match long edges and fold border pattern in half; crease firmly to create center line (shown with grey solid line). Match short edges and fold border pattern in half; crease firmly to create center line (shown with black solid line). Fold ends of border pattern $9^1/_4$" from each end; crease firmly (shown with black solid line). Divide the center section (the grey area in **Fig. 1**) into 10 equal parts; crease (shown with black dashed lines.)

2. Refer to **Fig. 2** to place a mark $2^5/_8$" from the horizontal center line on each of the creases (shown in red). Use a curved ruler or draw freehand a smooth gentle curve connecting the marks. Cut the pattern along the curved line. Discard the inside edge of the pattern.

3. With right sides facing up, place 1 white **middle border** on top of 1 medium green **middle border**. Pin borders together along edges to prevent shifting while sewing. Matching straight edge of pattern to outside edge of border, lay the freezer paper border pattern on top of the pinned borders; iron in place. Using the freezer paper border as a guide, stitch along the curved edge through both layers.

Fig. 1

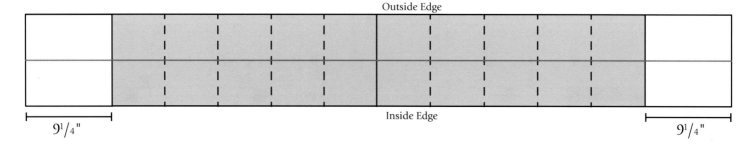

Fig. 2

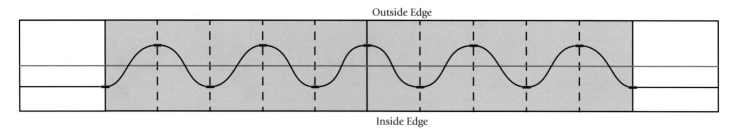

4. Remove pattern and trim the white fabric away from the outside edge by cutting approximately $1/4$" from the stitched curve line (**Fig. 3**). Turn border over. Trim the medium green fabric away from the inside edge by cutting approximately $1/4$" from the stitched curve line.

5. Repeat Steps 3-4 for remaining borders.

APPLIQUÉING THE MIDDLE BORDERS

1. Cut **bias strip** for vine into 4 pieces approximately 106" long. Matching wrong sides, fold each bias strip in half lengthwise. Stitch $1/4$" from the raw edges. Centering seam allowance on back, press vine flat. Trim seam allowance if necessary. Using a $1/2$" bias pressing bar makes pressing faster and easier.

2. Center the vine over the raw edge of the scalloped line of 1 border, easing along the curves and extending the ends into the corners. Leaving ends loose, pin or glue vine in place. The ends will be appliquéd in place after all borders are joined to the quilt. Refer to **Blanket Stitch Appliqué**, page 86, and use green embroidery thread (if desired) to stitch vine in place.

3. Repeat Step 2 with remaining borders.

4. Position and stitch leaves in place on border in same manner as vine. Leave some leaves off at the corners to be stitched in place after the borders are joined to the quilt.

ADDING THE MIDDLE AND OUTER BORDERS

1. Refer to **Adding Mitered Borders**, page 88, to sew middle borders to quilt top. The border curves should align in the corners but if they are slightly off it is okay because the vine ends will cover them.

2. Position the vine ends, overlapping and trimming them as needed in the corners. Fold under the ends and stitch in place. Add any remaining leaves.

3. Sew **outer borders** to quilt top in same manner as middle borders.

COMPLETING THE QUILT

1. Follow **Quilting**, page 89, to mark, layer, and quilt. Our quilt is machine quilted with the Emerald Isle quilting motif in the Block B's and curved lines on each side of each small square in Block A's and Block B's. There is stipple quilting around the Emerald Isle motif and in the middle border. There are parallel lines stitched in the inner border and along each edge of the outer border. There are diamonds quilted along each outer border.

2. Sew **piping strips** together using a diagonal seam (**Fig. 4**). Matching **wrong** sides, press strip in half lengthwise.

3. Tie a knot in 1 end of the cord. Using thread to match piping, lay the cord in the crease of the piping strip. Using a zipper foot or piping foot, stitch next to the piping (seam allowance should be to the right and the edge of the foot should be up against the cord. Stitch the entire length of the piping. Trim the piping seam allowance to $1/4$". **Optional:** Use Susan Cleveland's Groovin' Piping Trimming Tool.

Fig. 3

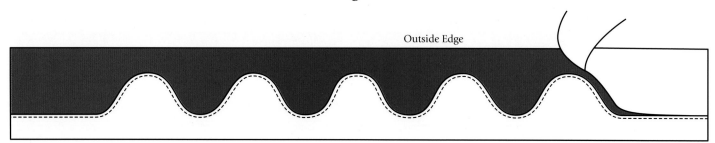

Outside Edge

Inside Edge

4. Cut piping into 4 equal lengths. Aligning the raw edge of the piping with the edge of the quilt top and allowing the ends of the piping to hang off the edge at beginning and end, sew the piping, one side at a time, to the quilt sandwich. When all piping is attached, trim the ends even with the quilt top.

5. Sew **binding strips** together using a diagonal seam (see **Fig. 4**). Follow **Attaching Binding with Mitered Corners**, page 93, to attach binding or use instructions included with Groovin' Piping Trimming Tool.

Fig. 4

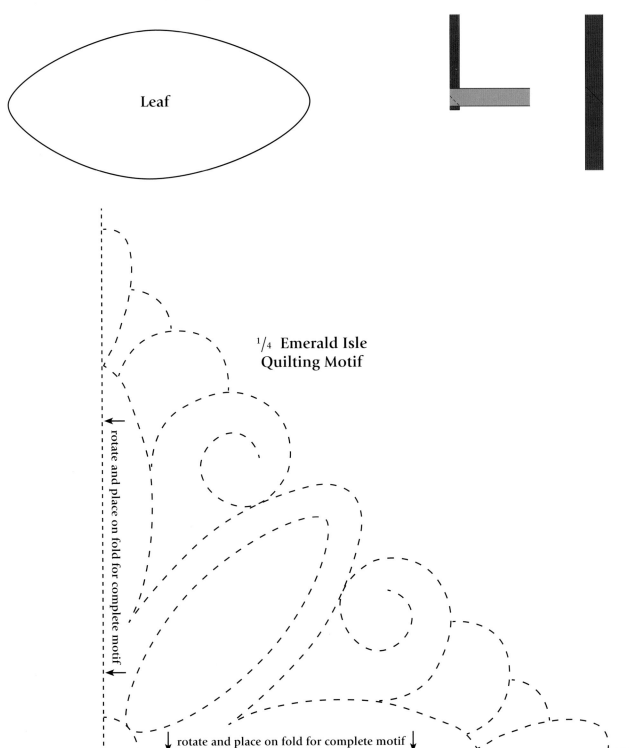

Leaf

¹/₄ **Emerald Isle Quilting Motif**

rotate and place on fold for complete motif

rotate and place on fold for complete motif

Finished Quilt Size: 87" x 99" (221 cm x 251 cm)
Finished Block Size: 12" x 12" (30 cm x 30 cm)

YARDAGE REQUIREMENTS

Yardage is based on 43"/44" (109 cm/112 cm)
wide fabric with a usable width of 40" (102 cm).

- 1¼ yds (1.1 m) of multi-color print fabric for outer border, blocks, and leaves
- 1 yd (91 cm) of black print fabric for binding, blocks, and leaves
- 1 yd (91 cm) of burgundy print fabric for vine, blocks, and leaves
- 3⅛ yds (2.9 m) of cream print #1 fabric for appliqué border and blocks (lighter of 2 border prints)
- 3 yds (2.7 m) of cream print #2 fabric for appliqué border and blocks
- ¾ yd (69 cm) *each* of cream print #3 and cream print #4 fabric for blocks
- 4⅛ yds (3.8 m) *total* of 13 assorted print fabrics or 14 assorted fat quarters
- 8 yds (7.3 m) of fabric for backing

You will also need:

95" x 107" (241 cm x 272 cm) piece of batting
No-melt Mylar Template Plastic
Optional: Clear monofilament thread
Optional: ½" (13 mm) bias pressing bar

CUTTING THE PIECES

*Follow **Rotary Cutting**, page 81, to cut fabric. Cut all strips across the selvage-to-selvage width of the fabric unless otherwise specified. Outer Borders include extra length for "insurance" and will be trimmed after assembling quilt top center. All measurements include ¼" seam allowances. Use pattern, page 27, and follow **Making and Using Templates**, page 84, Step 1, to make template for the leaf pattern.*

From multi-color print fabric:
- Cut 10 strips 3½"w. Sew strips together end to end and recut into 2 **side outer borders** 3½" x 96½" and 2 **top/bottom outer borders** 3½" x 90½".

From black print fabric:
- Cut 10 **binding strips** 2¼" wide.

From burgundy print fabric:
- Cut a 27" square of fabric. Refer to **Making A Continuous Bias Strip**, page 92, to make **bias strip** for vine 1½" x 400".

From cream #1 print fabric:
- Cut 2 strips 3⅞"w. From this strip, cut 16 squares 3⅞" x 3⅞". Cut each square *once* diagonally to make 32 **small triangles**.
- Cut 2 strips 7¼"w. From this strip, cut 8 squares 7¼" x 7¼". Cut each square *twice* diagonally to make 32 **large triangles**.
- Cut 2 *lengthwise* **side appliqué borders** 10½" x 92½".
- Cut 2 *lengthwise* **top/bottom appliqué borders** 10½" x 80½".

Continued on page 24.

From cream #2 print fabric:
- Cut 1 strip 3⁷/₈"w. From this strip, cut 10 squares 3⁷/₈" x 3⁷/₈". Cut each square *once* diagonally to make 20 **small triangles**.
- Cut 1 strip 7¹/₄"w. From this strip, cut 5 squares 7¹/₄" x 7¹/₄". Cut each square *twice* diagonally to make 20 **large triangles**.
- Cut 2 *lengthwise* **side appliqué borders** 10¹/₂" x 92¹/₂".
- Cut 2 *lengthwise* **top/bottom appliqué borders** 10¹/₂" x 80¹/₂".

From cream #3 print fabric:
- Cut 2 strips 3⁷/₈"w. From these strips, cut 20 squares 3⁷/₈" x 3⁷/₈". Cut each square *once* diagonally to make 40 **small triangles**.
- Cut 2 strips 7¹/₄"w. From these strips, cut 10 squares 7¹/₄" x 7¹/₄". Cut each square *twice* diagonally to make 40 **large triangles**.

From cream #4 print fabric:
- Cut 2 strips 3⁷/₈"w. From these strips, cut 14 squares 3⁷/₈" x 3⁷/₈". Cut each square *once* diagonally to make 28 **small triangles**.
- Cut 2 strips 7¹/₄"w. From these strips, cut 7 squares 7¹/₄" x 7¹/₄". Cut each square *twice* diagonally to make 28 **large triangles**.

From assorted print fabrics (also include remaining multi-color print, black print, and burgundy print):
- Cut 90 **strips** 1⁷/₈" x 21".
- Cut 30 **squares** 4³/₄" x 4³/₄".
- Refer to **Preparing Blanket Stitch or Zigzag Stitch Appliqués**, page 85, and use template to cut 112 **leaves**.

ASSEMBLING THE BLOCKS
Follow Machine Piecing, page 82, and Pressing, page 83, to assemble the quilt top. For each Block, use matching small and large triangles.

1. Using a scant ¹/₄" seam allowance, sew 3 assorted **strips** together to make **Strip Set A**. Strip Set A should measure 4³/₄"w. Cut across Strip Set A at 4³/₄" intervals to make **Unit 1**. Make 4 Unit 1's.

2. Sew 1 **Unit 1** and 2 **large triangles** together to make **Unit 2**. Make 2 Unit 2's.
3. Sew 1 **square** and 2 **Unit 1's** together to make **Unit 3**.
4. Sew 2 Unit 2's and **Unit 3** together to make **Unit 4**.
5. Sew 1 **small triangle** to each corner of Unit 4 to make 1 **Block**.
6. Repeat Steps 1-5 to make a total of 30 Blocks.

ASSEMBLING THE QUILT TOP CENTER
Refer to photo for placement.

1. Sew 5 Blocks together to make a Row. Make 6 Rows. Press seam allowances in odd number rows in one direction; press seam allowances in even number rows in opposite direction.

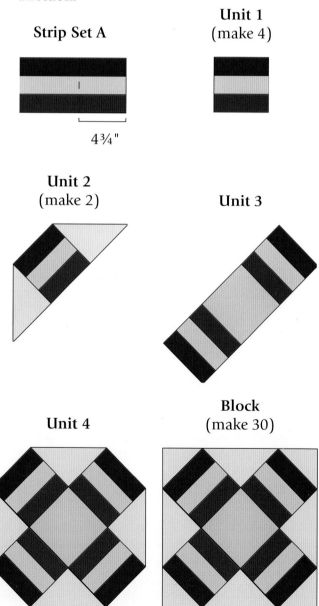

Strip Set A

4³/₄"

Unit 1
(make 4)

Unit 2
(make 2)

Unit 3

Unit 4

Block
(make 30)

2. Sew Rows together. Press seam allowances toward bottom of quilt top center. Quilt top center should measure $60^1/2$" x $72^1/2$" including seam allowances.

PREPARING THE BORDERS

1. To create top/bottom border pattern, cut a strip of freezer paper $10^1/2$" x $80^1/2$". Referring to **Fig. 1**, match long edges and fold border pattern in half; crease firmly to create center line (shown with grey solid line). Match short edges and fold border pattern in half; crease firmly to create center line (shown with black solid line). Fold ends of border pattern $10^1/4$" from each end; crease firmly (shown with black solid line). Divide the center section (the grey area) into 6 equal parts; crease (shown with black dashed lines).

2. Refer to **Fig. 2** to place a mark 1" from the horizontal center line on each of the creases (shown in red). Use a curved ruler or draw freehand a smooth gentle curve connecting the marks. Cut the pattern along the curved line. Discard the inside edge of the pattern.

3. (*Note: The cream #1 print fabric is the lighter of the 2 border fabrics and will be positioned next to the quilt top center.*) With right sides facing up, place 1 cream #1 print **top/bottom appliqué border** on top of 1 cream #2 print **top/bottom appliqué border**. Pin borders together along edges to prevent shifting while sewing. Matching straight edge of pattern to outside edge of border, lay the freezer paper border pattern on top of the pinned borders; iron in place. Using the freezer paper border as a guide, stitch along the curved edge through both layers.

4. Remove pattern and trim the cream #1 print border (the lighter fabric) away from the outside edge by cutting approximately $1/4$" from the stitched curve line (**Fig. 3**). Turn border over. Trim the cream #2 print fabric away from inside edge by cutting approximately $1/4$" from the stitched curve line.

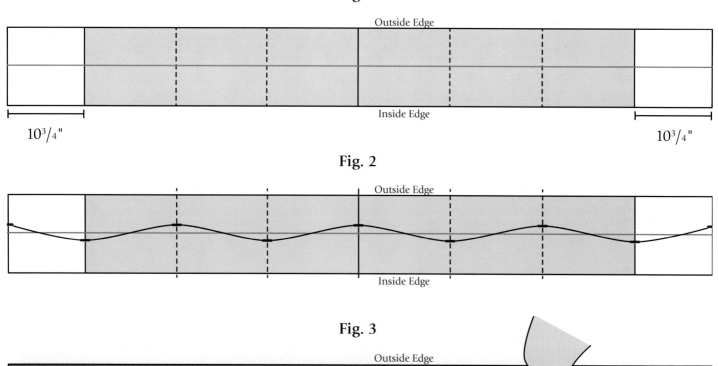

Fig. 1

Outside Edge

Inside Edge

$10^3/4$" $10^3/4$"

Fig. 2

Outside Edge

Inside Edge

Fig. 3

Outside Edge

Inside Edge

5. Repeat Steps 3-4 for bottom border.
6. For side borders, repeat Steps 1-4, cutting a strip of freezer paper $10^1/_2$" x $92^1/_2$" and dividing the center section into 8 parts.

APPLIQUÉING THE BORDERS
1. Cut **bias strip** for vine into 4 pieces approximately 100" long. Matching wrong sides, fold each bias strip in half lengthwise. Stitch $^1/_4$" from raw edges. Centering seam allowance on back, press vine flat. Trim seam allowance if necessary. Using a $^1/_2$" bias pressing bar makes pressing faster and easier.
2. Center the vine over the raw edge of the scalloped line of border, easing along the curves and extending the ends into the corners (**Fig. 4**). Leaving ends loose, pin or glue vine in place. These ends will be appliquéd in place after all borders are joined to the quilt. Use a narrow zigzag stitch and monofilament thread (if desired) to stitch vine in place.
3. Repeat Step 2 with remaining borders.

Fig. 4

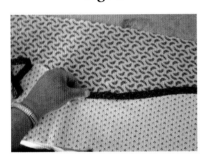

4. Position and stitch leaves in place on the borders in same manner as vine. Leave some leaves off at the corners to be stitched in place after the borders are joined to the quilt.

ADDING THE BORDERS
1. Refer to **Adding Mitered Borders**, page 88, to sew borders to quilt top center. The border curves should align in the corners but if they are slightly off it is okay because the vine will cover them.
2. Position the vine ends, overlapping and trimming them as needed in the corners. Fold under the ends and stitch in place. Add any remaining leaves.
3. Refer to **Adding Squared Borders**, page 88, to add **side** then **top** and **bottom outer borders** to the quilt top.

COMPLETING THE QUILT
1. Follow **Quilting**, page 89, to mark, layer, and quilt as desired. Quilt shown is machine quilted with a flower in the center and feathers in the triangles of each Block. There is stipple quilting in the border and perpendicular double lines, spaced approximately $1^1/_2$" apart, in the outer border.
2. Sew **binding strips** together using a diagonal seam (**Fig. 5**) to make a continuous binding strip.
3. Follow **Attaching Binding With Mitered Corners**, page 93, to attach binding.

Fig. 5

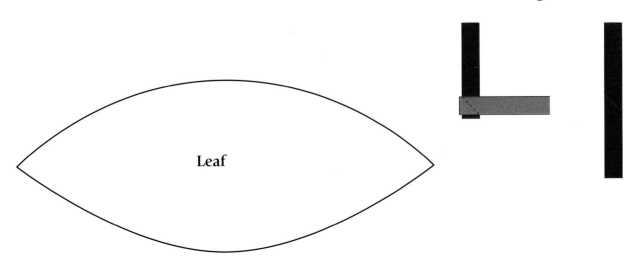

Leaf

Finished Quilt Size: 85³/₄" x 108³/₈" (218 cm x 275 cm)
Finished Block Size: 14" x 14" (36 cm x 36 cm)

YARDAGE REQUIREMENTS

Yardage is based on 43"/44" (109 cm/112 cm) wide fabric with a usable width of 40" (102 cm). A fat quarter measures approximately 18" x 21" (46 cm x 53 cm).

- 5 yds (4.6 m) of floral print fabric
- 5⁵/₈ yds (5.1 m) of tan print fabric
- 3³/₈ yds (3.1 m) of off-white print fabric
- ¹/₄ yd (23 cm) of dark green print fabric
- 1⁵/₈ yds (1.5 m) *total* of assorted green print fabrics or 6 assorted fat quarters
- 1¹/₄ yds (1.1 m) of assorted gold print fabrics or 4 assorted fat quarters
- 1¹/₂ yds (1.4 m) *total* of assorted pink, blue, and grey print fabrics or 6-8 assorted fat quarters
- 7⁷/₈ yds (7.2 m) of fabric for backing

You will also need:

- 93³/₄" x 116³/₈" (238 cm x 296 cm) piece of batting
- Template plastic
- That Patchwork Place® 8¹/₂" x 11" (22 cm x 28 cm) papers for foundation piecing

CUTTING THE PIECES

*Follow **Rotary Cutting**, page 81, to cut fabric. Borders include extra length for "insurance" and will be trimmed after assembling quilt top center. All measurements include ¹/₄" seam allowances. Use patterns, page 33, and follow **Making and Using Templates**, page 84, to make a piecing template for piece A and an appliqué template for piece B.*

From floral print fabric:
- Cut 11 **binding strips** 2¹/₂"w.
- Cut 3 strips 14¹/₂"w. From these strips, cut 48 **sashing strips** 2¹/₂" x 14¹/₂".
- Cut 2 *lengthwise* top/bottom borders 7¹/₂" x 89¹/₄".
- Cut 2 *lengthwise* side borders 7¹/₂" x 97⁷/₈".

From remaining width:
- Use appliqué template to cut 18 **compass centers (B)**.

From tan print fabric:
- Cut 3 squares 24¹/₂" x 24¹/₂". Cut each square *twice* diagonally to make 12 **side setting triangles**. You will use 10 and have 2 left over. These are over-cut and will be trimmed after assembling the quilt top center.
- Cut 2 squares 14" x 14". Cut each square *once* diagonally to make 4 **corner setting triangles**. These are over-cut and will be trimmed after assembling the quilt top center.
- Use piecing template to cut 72 **block backgrounds (A)**.

From off-white print fabric:
- Cut 29 strips 4"w. From these strips, cut 288 **rectangles** 3³/₄" x 4" for paper piecing the compass background, pieces #2 and #3.

From dark green print fabric:
- Cut 2 strips 2¹/₂"w. From these strips, cut 31 **sashing posts** 2¹/₂" x 2¹/₂".

From assorted green print fabrics or 6 assorted fat quarters:
- Cut 18 sets of 8 matching **rectangles** 2¹/₂" x 5¹/₂" for paper piecing compass point #1.

Continued on page 30.

From assorted gold print fabrics or 4 assorted fat quarters:
- Cut 18 sets of 4 matching **rectangles** $3^1/4$" x 6" for paper piecing compass point #4.

From assorted pink, blue, and grey print fabrics or 6-8 assorted fat quarters:
- Cut 18 sets of 4 matching **rectangles** $3^1/2$" x $6^1/2$" for paper piecing compass point #5.

ASSEMBLING THE BLOCKS

1. Photocopy Units C and D, page 32, onto foundation piecing paper. Make 72 copies.
2. Refer to **Foundation Paper Piecing**, page 83, to stitch and flip **rectangles** in numerical order for Units C and D.
3. Sew Units D and C together (**Fig. 1**) to make 4 Quarter Sections. Sew 4 Quarter Sections together; press.
4. Refer to **Needle-Turn Appliqué**, page 84, to appliqué **compass center (B)** to compass (**Fig. 2**), being careful not to cover points.
5. Mark diagonal lines in seam allowances of **block backgrounds (A)**. Sew 4 block backgrounds (A) together along short edges. Matching main compass points #5 with the seamlines on background and compass points #4 with marked diagonal lines, pin compass to background. Add additional pins as necessary. Sew with background on top, easing as necessary. Press seam allowances toward background. Remove paper foundations. Block should measure $14^1/2$" x $14^1/2$" including seam allowances. Make 18 Blocks.

ASSEMBLING THE QUILT TOP

*Refer to **Machine Piecing**, page 82, and **Pressing**, page 83, and use a $^1/4$" seam allowance. Refer to **Quilt Assembly Diagram**, for placement.*

1. Lay out **Blocks**, **sashing strips**, **sashing posts**, **side setting triangles**, and **corner setting triangles** for Quilt Top Center.
2. Sew pieces together in diagonal rows. Add corner setting triangles to each corner.

3. Trim outer edges of quilt top center $^1/4$" beyond outer points of sashing posts.
4. Refer to **Adding Squared Borders**, page 88, to add **side**, then **top** and **bottom borders** to quilt top.

Unit C
(Make 4)

Unit D
(Make 4)

Fig. 1

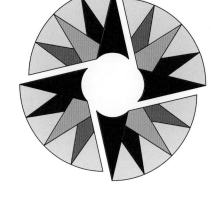

Fig. 2

Block (make 18)

COMPLETING THE QUILT

Fig. 3

1. Follow **Quilting**, page 89, to mark, layer, and quilt as desired. Quilt shown is machine quilted with an all-over flower and vine pattern.
2. Sew **binding strips** together using a diagonal seam (**Fig. 3**) to make a continuous binding strip.
3. Follow **Attaching Binding With Mitered Corners**, page 93, to attach binding.

Quilt Assembly Diagram

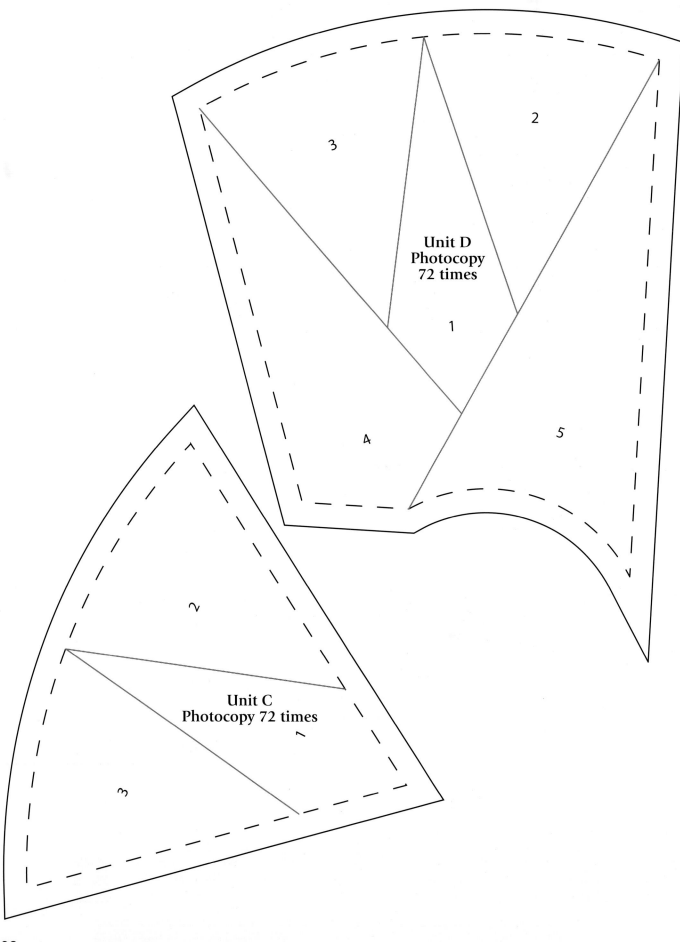

Unit D
Photocopy
72 times

2

3

1

4

5

Unit C
Photocopy 72 times

2

1

3

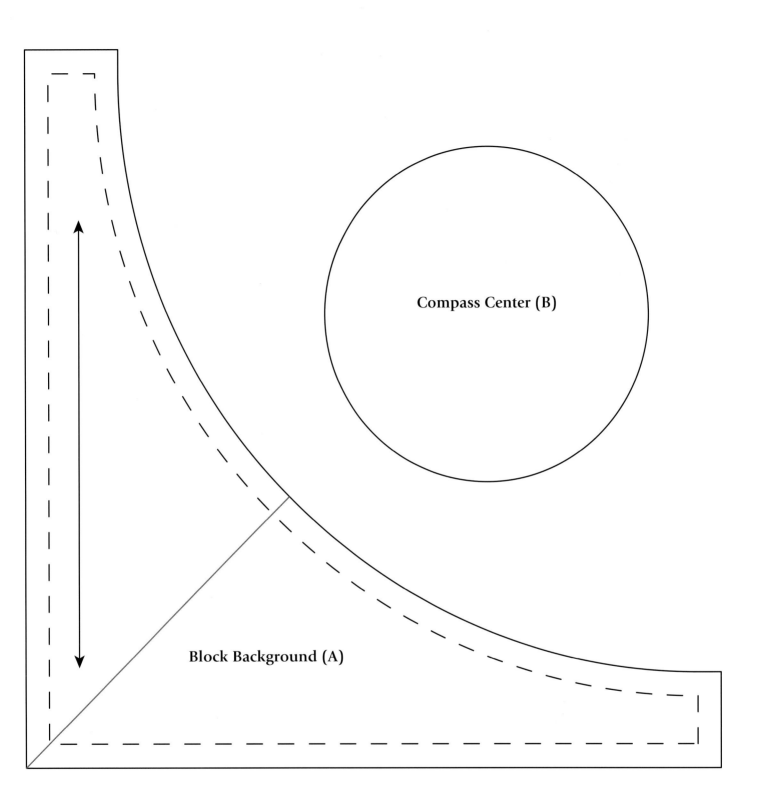

Compass Center (B)

Block Background (A)

HOMEWARD BOUND

Finished Quilt Size: 82¹/₂" x 90⁷/₈" (210 cm x 231 cm)
Finished Block Size: 6" x 6" (15 cm x 15 cm)

YARDAGE REQUIREMENTS

Yardage is based on 43"/44" (109 cm/112 cm) wide fabric with a usable width of 40" (102 cm).

2¹/₂ yds (2.3 m) of tan/red small floral print fabric for setting triangles and inner border

2¹/₂ yds (2.3 m) of brown print fabric for outer border and binding

³/₄ yd (69 cm) of dark blue print fabric for vine

2¹/₈ yds (1.9 m) *total* of assorted light/medium print fabrics for blocks

3¹/₄ yds (3.3 m) *total* of assorted dark print fabrics for blocks and leaves

7⁵/₈ yds (7 m) of fabric for backing

You will also need:

90¹/₂" x 99" (230 cm x 251 cm) piece of batting

Template plastic

Optional: ¹/₂" (13 mm) bias pressing bar

CUTTING THE PIECES

*Follow **Rotary Cutting**, page 81, to cut fabric. Borders include extra length for "insurance" and will be trimmed after assembling quilt top center. The side setting triangles and corner setting triangles are over-cut and will be trimmed after assembly. All measurements include ¹/₄" seam allowances. Use pattern, page 38, and follow **Making and Using Templates**, page 84, to make appliqué template for the leaf.*

From tan/red small floral print fabric:
- Cut 2 *lengthwise* **side inner borders** 6¹/₂" x 72³/₈".
- Cut 2 *lengthwise* **top/bottom inner borders** 6¹/₂" x 76".

From the remaining width:
- Cut 3 strips 10"w. From these strips, cut 7 squares 10" x 10". Cut each square *twice* diagonally to make 28 **side setting triangles**. You will use 26 triangles and have 2 left over.
- Cut 2 squares 5³/₈" x 5³/₈". Cut each square *once* diagonally to make 4 **corner setting triangles**.

From brown print fabric:
- Cut 2 *lengthwise* **side outer borders** 5¹/₂" x 84³/₈".
- Cut 2 *lengthwise* **top/bottom outer borders** 5¹/₂" x 86".
- Cut 5 *lengthwise* **binding strips** 2¹/₂" x 90".

From dark blue print fabric:
- Cut 1 square 24" x 24". Refer to **Making a Continuous Bias Strip**, page 92, to cut 1 **bias strip** for vine 1¹/₂" x 300".

From assorted light/medium print fabrics (including remaining tan/red small floral print fabrics):

- Cut 49 matching sets of 3 **squares** 3" x 3" and 3 squares $2^7/_8$" x $2^7/_8$". Cut the $2^7/_8$" x $2^7/_8$" squares *once* diagonally to make 6 **small triangles**.

From assorted dark print fabrics (including remaining brown print and dark blue print fabrics:

- Cut 49 matching sets of 1 square $6^7/_8$" x $6^7/_8$" and 3 **squares** 3" x 3". Cut the larger square *once* diagonally to make 2 **large triangles**.
- Use template to cut 132 **leaves**.

ASSEMBLING THE BLOCKS

Follow Machine Piecing, page 82, and Pressing, page 83, and use a $^1/_4$" seam allowance.

1. Draw a diagonal line on wrong side of each assorted light/medium print **square**. With right sides together, place 1 light/medium print square on top of 1 dark print **square**. Stitch $^1/_4$" from each side of drawn line (**Fig. 1**).

2. Cut along drawn line and press open, pressing seam allowances toward darker fabric to make 2 **Triangle-Squares**. Make 49 sets of 6 matching Triangle-Squares. Trim each Triangle-Square to $2^1/_2$" x $2^1/_2$".

3. Refer to **Fig. 2** to sew 3 matching light/medium **triangles** and 3 Triangles-Squares together to make **Unit 1**. Make 49 sets of 2 matching Unit 1's.

4. Sew matching **large triangle** to Unit 1 to make **Block**. Make 49 sets of 2 matching Blocks.

Fig. 1

Triangle-Squares
(make 49 sets of 6)

Fig. 2

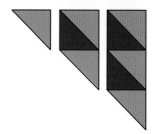

Unit 1
(make 49 sets of 2)

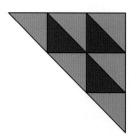

Block
(make 49 sets of 2)

ASSEMBLING THE QUILT TOP
Refer to Assembly Diagram, page 39.

1. Sew **side setting triangles** and Blocks together in diagonal rows. Sew rows together. Sew **corner setting triangles** to corners. Trim quilt top edges 1/4" from corners of blocks.

2. Refer to **Adding Squared Borders**, page 88, to add **side**, then **top** and **bottom inner borders** to quilt top.

3. In same manner, sew **side**, then **top** and **bottom outer borders** to quilt top.

ADDING THE APPLIQUÉS

1. Matching wrong sides, fold **bias strip** for vine in half. Stitch $1/4$" from raw edge. Trim seam allowances to $1/8$" (**Fig. 3**). Press vine flat, centering seam allowances on back so raw edge isn't visible from front. Using a $1/2$" bias pressing bar makes pressing faster and easier.
2. Pin vine to inner border, trimming and tucking ends under as needed.
3. Refer to **Blind Stitch**, page 95, to stitch vine in place.
4. Pin leaves to inner border. Refer to **Needle-Turn Appliqué**, page 84, to stitch leaves in place.

COMPLETING THE QUILT

1. Follow **Quilting**, page 89, to mark, layer, and quilt as desired. Quilt shown is machine quilted with an all-over feather design in the blocks. The vine and leaves are echo quilted. The outer border is filled with channel quilting $3/4$" apart, perpendicular to the border seams.
2. Sew **binding strips** together using a diagonal seam (**Fig. 4**) to make a continuous binding strip.
3. Follow **Attaching Binding With Mitered Corners**, page 93, to attach binding.

Fig. 3

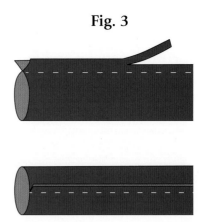

Fig. 4

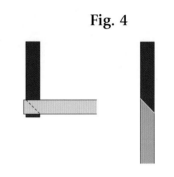

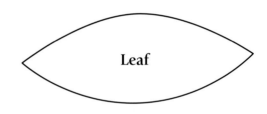

Leaf

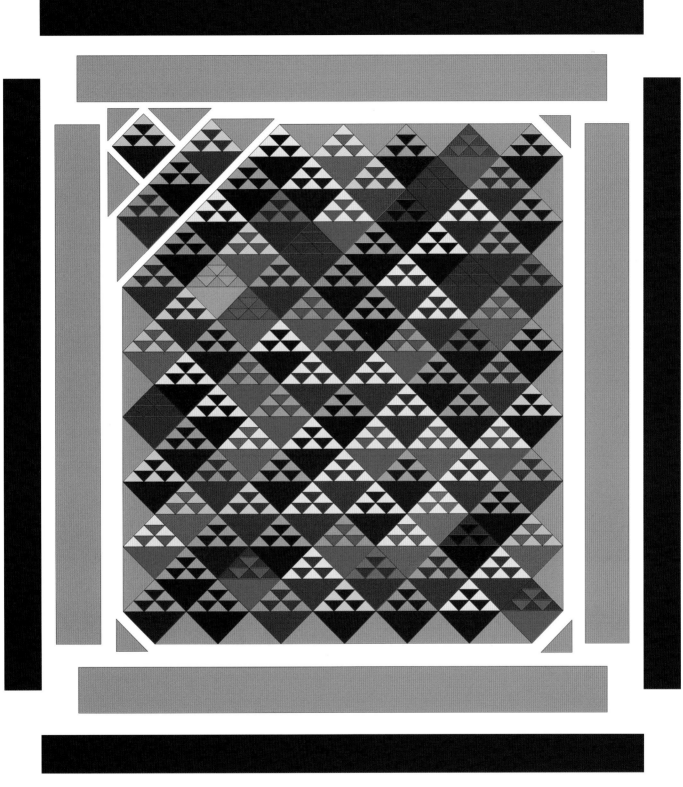

PRESSED FLOWERS

Finished Quilt Size: 49" x 49" (124 cm x 124 cm)
Finished Block Size: 12" x 12" (30 cm x 30 cm)

YARDAGE REQUIREMENTS

Yardage is based on 43"/44" (109 cm/112 cm)
wide fabric with a usable width of 40" (102 cm).

- $1^1/_4$ yds (1.1 m) of cream print fabric
- 1 fat quarter of olive green print fabric
- $^1/_2$ yd (46 cm) ***each*** of 6 coordinating print fabrics
- $3^1/_4$ yds (3 m) of fabric for backing
- $^1/_2$ yd (46 cm) ***total*** of assorted fabrics for binding

You will also need:

- 57" x 57" (145 cm x 145 cm) piece of batting
- Template plastic
- **Optional:** $^3/_8$" (10 cm) bias pressing bar

CUTTING THE PIECES

*Follow **Rotary Cutting**, page 81, to cut fabric.*
Background squares are overcut and will be trimmed
after appliqués are added. All measurements include
$^1/_4$" seam allowances. Use patterns, page 44, and
*follow **Making and Using Templates**, page 84, to*
make 1 appliqué template for each of patterns A-D.

From cream print fabric:

- Cut 3 strips $13^1/_2$" wide. From these strips, cut 9 **background squares** $13^1/_2$" x $13^1/_2$".

From olive green print fabric:

- Cut 6 **strips** $1^1/_4$" x 21".

From the 6 coordinating print fabrics:

- Cut a ***total*** of 72 assorted **rectangles** (**E**) $2^1/_2$" x $6^1/_2$".
- Cut a ***total*** of 36 assorted **squares** (**F**) $2^1/_2$" x $2^1/_2$".
- Use template to cut a ***total*** of 9 sets of 4 matching **flowers** (**A**).
- Use template to cut a ***total*** of 9 sets of 8 matching **leaves** (**B**).
- Use template to cut a ***total*** of 9 sets of 8 matching **leaves** (**C**).
- Use template to cut a ***total*** of 9 circles (**D**).

From assorted fabrics for binding:

- Cut 6 assorted **binding strips** $2^1/_4$" w.

ASSEMBLING THE PRESSED FLOWER BLOCKS

1. Finger-press **background square** in half vertically, horizontally, and diagonally to create placement guides for appliqués.
2. Match wrong sides and fold each olive green **strip** in half lengthwise. Stitch $1/4$" from raw edges. Pressing seam allowances to one side, press tube flat. Trim seam allowances if necessary. Using a $1/4$" bias pressing bar makes pressing faster and easier.
3. Cut tubes into 18 stems approximately 7" long. Center stems along diagonally pressed lines; pin in place.
4. Refer to **Blind Stitch**, page 95, to stitch stems in place.
5. Pin **flowers (A)**, **leaves (B and C)**, and **circles (D)** to background square. Refer to **Needle-Turn Appliqué**, page 84, to stitch appliqués in place.
6. Centering design, trim background square to $12^{1}/_{2}$" x $12^{1}/_{2}$" to make **Block**. Make 9 Blocks.

Block (make 9)

Row (make 3)

ASSEMBLING THE QUILT TOP CENTER

*Follow **Machine Piecing**, page 82, and **Pressing**, page 83, and use a $1/4$" seam allowance.*

1. Sew 3 Blocks together to make a **Row**. Make 3 Rows. If you have used a stripe background fabric as Nancy did, rotate alternate blocks to create a woven look.
2. Sew the Rows together to make quilt top center.
3. Sew 9 **squares** (F) together to make a **9-Patch Block**. Make 4 9-Patch Blocks.
4. Sew 18 **rectangles** (E) together to make **Border**. Make 4 Borders.
5. Sew 1 Border to top and bottom of quilt top center. Press seam allowances toward borders.
6. Sew 1 9-Patch Block to each end of remaining borders.
7. Sew remaining Borders to quilt top center.

9-Patch Block (make 4)

Border (make 4)

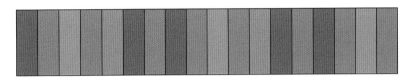

Quilt Top Diagram

COMPLETING THE QUILT

1. Follow **Quilting**, page 89, to mark, layer, and quilt as desired. Quilt shown is machine quilted with meandering quilting in the block backgrounds around all appliqués. The borders are quilted in the ditch and lengthwise through the center of each square and rectangle.
2. Sew **binding strips** together using a diagonal seam (**Fig. 1**) to make a continuous binding strip.
3. Follow **Attaching Binding With Mitered Corners**, page 93, to attach binding.

Fig. 1

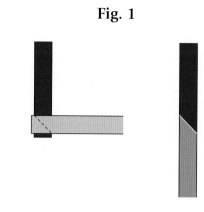

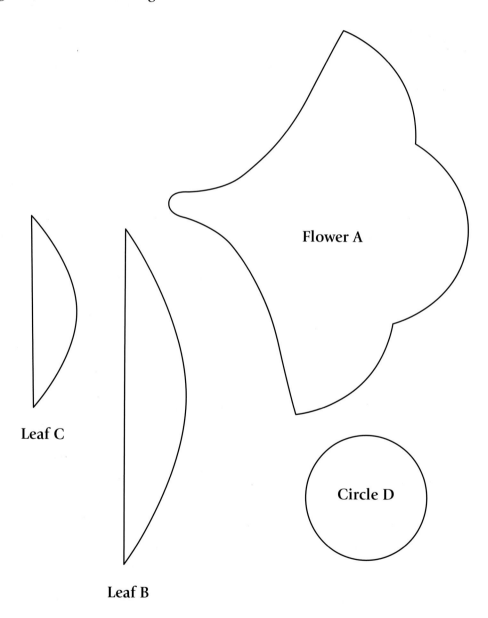

Flower A

Leaf C

Circle D

Leaf B

MARKET BLOSSOMS

Finished Quilt Size: 37" x 37" (94 cm x 94 cm)

YARDAGE REQUIREMENTS

Yardage is based on 43"/44" (109 cm/112 cm) wide fabric with a usable width of 40" (102 cm). A fat quarter measures approximately 18" x 21" (46 cm x 53 cm).

- ³/₄ yd (69 cm) of butter cream tone-on-tone print fabric
- 1 fat quarter of black floral print fabric
- 1 fat quarter of green print fabric
- 1 fat quarter of red plaid fabric
- ⁵/₈ yd (57 cm) of red print fabric
- ⁵/₈ yd (57 cm) of multi-color stripe fabric
- 2¹/₂ yds (2.3 m) of fabric for backing

You will also need:

- 45" x 45" (114 cm x 114 cm) piece of batting
- Template plastic

CUTTING THE PIECES

*Follow **Rotary Cutting**, page 81, to cut fabric. Middle borders include extra length for "insurance" and will be trimmed after assembling the quilt top center. All measurements include ¹/₄" seam allowances. Use patterns, page 51, and follow **Making and Using Templates**, page 84, to make 1 appliqué template for **each** of patterns A - G.*

From butter cream tone-on-tone print fabric:
- Cut 1 strip 7¹/₂" wide. From this strip, cut 4 **large squares** 7¹/₂" x 7¹/₂".
- Cut 1 **background square** 13¹/₂" x 13¹/₂".
- Cut 2 squares 8¹/₄" x 8¹/₄". Cut each square *twice* diagonally to make 8 **triangles**.

From black floral print fat quarter:
- Cut 1 strip 8¹/₄" wide. From this strip, cut 2 squares 8¹/₄" x 8¹/₄". Cut each square *twice* diagonally to make 8 **triangles**.
- Use template to cut 4 **flower petals** (C).
- Use template to cut 4 **diamonds** (E).

Continued on page 48.

From green print fat quarter:
- Cut 1 **strip** 1" x 18".
- Cut 2 strips 5^1/$_2$" wide. From these strips, cut 4 **medium squares** 5^1/$_2$" x 5^1/$_2$".
- Cut 1 strip 3^1/$_2$" wide. From this strip, cut 4 **small squares** 3^1/$_2$" x 3^1/$_2$".
- Use template to cut 4 **flower bases (D)**.
- Use template to cut 8 **leaves (F)**.

From red plaid fat quarter:
- Cut 1 strip 8^1/$_4$" wide. From this strip, cut 2 squares 8^1/$_4$" x 8^1/$_4$". Cut each square *twice* diagonally to make 8 **triangles**.
- Use template to cut 8 **flower petals (B)**.
- Use template to cut 1 **circle (G)**.

From red print fabric:
- Cut 2 **side middle borders** 1^1/$_2$" x 32^1/$_2$".
- Cut 2 **top/bottom middle borders** 1^1/$_2$" x 34^1/$_2$".
- Cut 5 **binding strips** 2^1/$_4$" wide.
- Use template to cut 4 **flower petals (A)**.

From multi-color stripe fabric:
- Cut 2 **side inner borders** 1^1/$_2$" x 12^1/$_2$".
- Cut 2 **top/bottom inner borders** 1^1/$_2$" x 14^1/$_2$".
- Cut 4 **outer borders** 3^1/$_2$" x 30^1/$_2$".

APPLIQUÉING THE BACKGROUND SQUARE

Refer to photo for placement.

1. To make the stems, match wrong sides and fold **strip** in half lengthwise. Stitch ^{1}/$_4$" from raw edges. Pressing seam allowances to one side, press tube flat. Trim seam allowances if necessary. Using a ^{1}/$_4$" bias pressing bar makes pressing faster and easier. Cut into 4 segments 4" long.

2. Finger-press **background square** in half vertically, horizontally, and diagonally to create placement guides for appliqués. Beginning with 1 end approximately ^{3}/$_8$" from the block's center, pin stems on the diagonal crease. Refer to **Blind Stitch**, page 95, to stitch stems in place.

3. Refer to **Needle-Turn Appliqué**, page 84, to stitch appliqués in alphabetical order. Press square from the wrong side. Centering design, trim background square to 12^1/$_2$" x 12^1/$_2$".

ADDING BORDERS

Follow Machine Piecing, page 82, and Pressing, page 83, and use a ¹/₄" seam allowance.

1. Sew **side inner borders** to sides of background square. Press seam allowances toward borders. Sew **top** and **bottom inner borders** to the background square to complete the quilt top center; press seam allowances toward borders.

2. Sew 2 butter cream tone-on-tone **triangles** and 1 **medium square** together to make **Unit 1**. Make 4 Unit 1's.

3. Sew 1 black floral **triangle** and 1 red plaid **triangle** together to make **Unit 2**. Make a total of 4 left Unit 2's and 4 right Unit 2's.

4. Sew 1 Unit 1, 1 left Unit 2, and 1 right Unit 2 together to make **Unit 3**. Make 4 Unit 3's.

5. Referring to photo and paying careful attention to the orientation, sew 1 Unit 3 to each side of the quilt top center. Sew 1 **large square** to each end of the 2 remaining Unit 3's. Press seam allowances toward the squares. Sew these to the top and bottom of the quilt top.

6. Refer to **Adding Squared Borders**, page 88, to sew **side middle borders** to the quilt top and then **top** and **bottom middle borders** to the quilt top. Press seam allowances toward the borders.

7. Sew 1 **outer border** to opposite sides of the quilt top. Sew **small squares** to each end of the remaining outer borders. Press seam allowances toward squares. Sew borders to top and bottom of the quilt top. Press seam allowances toward the borders.

COMPLETING THE QUILT

1. Follow **Quilting**, page 89, to mark, layer, and quilt as desired. Quilt shown is machine quilted with stipple quilting in the background square, outline quilting along each border, and feathers in the wide middle borders and small corner squares. There is channel quilting in the outer border approximately 1" apart.

2. Sew **binding strips** together using a diagonal seam (**Fig. 1**) to make a continuous binding strip.

3. Follow **Attaching Binding With Mitered Corners**, page 93, to attach binding.

Unit 1
(make 4)

Unit 2
(make 4 left and 4 right)

Unit 3
(make 4)

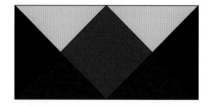

Fig. 1

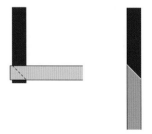

PATCHES OF BLUE

Finished Quilt Size: 55" x 73" (140 cm x 185 cm)
Finished Block Size: 9" x 9" (23 cm x 23 cm)

YARDAGE REQUIREMENTS

Yardage is based on 43"/44" (109 cm/112 cm) wide fabric with a usable width of 40" (102 cm). A fat eight measures approximately 9" x 21" (23 cm x 53 cm).

- $2^3/_8$ yds (2.2 m) of dark blue solid fabric
- $1^7/_8$ yds (1.7 m) *total* or 12 fat eighths of assorted light print fabrics
- $1^3/_8$ yds (1.3 m) *total* or 10 fat eighths of assorted dark blue print fabrics
- $^1/_4$ yd (23 cm) of light blue print fabric for birds
- $^1/_4$ yd (23 cm) *total* or 4 fat eighths of assorted medium blue print fabrics for leaves
- $^3/_4$ yd (69 cm) of blue plaid fabric for vine
- $4^1/_2$ yds (4.1 m) of fabric for backing

You will also need:

- 63" x 81" (160 cm x 206 cm) piece of batting
- Paper-backed fusible web
- **Optional:** $^1/_2$" (13 mm) bias pressing bar

CUTTING THE PIECES

*Follow **Rotary Cutting**, page 81, to cut fabric. Borders are cut exact length. All measurements include $^1/_4$" seam allowances.*

From dark blue solid fabric:
- Cut 3 strips $3^1/_2$"w. From these strips, cut 24 **small squares** $3^1/_2$" x $3^1/_2$".
- Cut 7 **binding strips** $2^1/_4$"w.
- Cut 4 *lengthwise* **borders** $9^1/_2$" x $54^1/_2$".

From assorted light print fabrics:
- Cut 72 **small squares** $3^1/_2$" x $3^1/_2$".
- Cut 24 **large squares** 4" x 4".

From assorted dark blue print fabrics:
- Cut 72 **small squares** $3^1/_2$" x $3^1/_2$".
- Cut 24 **large squares** 4" x 4".

From blue plaid fabric:
- Cut 22" x 22" square. Refer to **Making A Continuous Bias Strip**, page 92, to make bias strip $1^1/_2$" x 260" for vine.

CUTTING THE APPLIQUÉS

*Refer to **Preparing Fusible Appliqués**, page 85, and use patterns, pages 57-59, to prepare appliqués.*

From assorted light blue print fabrics:
- Cut 4 **corner flowers** (G).
- Cut 4 **corner leaves** (F).
- Cut 8 **large flowers** (A).
- Cut 16 **small flowers** (C).

From assorted dark blue print fabrics:
- Cut 8 **medium flowers** (B).
- Cut 24 **flower centers** (D).

From light blue print fabric for birds:
- Cut 4 **birds** (E).

From assorted medium blue print fabrics:
- Cut 18 **leaves** (H).

ASSEMBLING THE BLOCKS

*Follow **Machine Piecing**, page 82, and **Pressing**, page 83, and use a $1/4$" seam allowance.*

1. Draw a diagonal line on wrong side of each assorted light print **large square**. With right sides together, place 1 light print large square on top of 1 assorted dark print **large square**. Stitch seam $1/4$" from each side of drawn line (**Fig. 1**).

2. Cut along drawn line and press seam allowances toward darker fabric to make 2 **Triangle-Squares**. Make 48 assorted Triangle-Squares. Trim each Triangle-Square to $3^1/2$" x $3^1/2$".

3. Sew 2 Triangle-Squares, 3 light **small squares**, 3 dark **small squares**, and 1 solid blue **small square** together to make a **Block**. Make 24 Blocks.

ASSEMBLING THE QUILT TOP CENTER

*Refer to **Quilt Top Diagram**, for placement.*

1. Paying close attention to the orientation of the block, lay out Blocks in 6 Rows of 4 Blocks each.

2. Sew Blocks together into **Rows**. Press seam allowances in even numbered rows to the right. Press seam allowances in odd numbered rows to the left.

3. Sew Rows together to complete quilt top center. Quilt top center should measure $36^1/2$" x $54^1/2$" including seam allowances.

APPLIQUÉING THE BORDERS

1. Matching wrong sides, fold **bias strip** for vine in half. Stitch a scant $1/4$" from raw edge. Trim seam allowances to $1/8$". Press tube flat, centering seam allowances on back so raw edge isn't visible from front. Using a $1/2$" bias pressing bar makes pressing faster and easier. Cut vine into two 56" lengths and two 74" lengths.

2. Refer to **Border Diagrams**, page 56, to pin vine to **borders** according to placement guidelines, trimming and tucking ends under as needed. On side borders, leave vine ends longer than side borders. Refer to **Blind Stitch**, page 95, to stitch vine in place. Leave approximately 10" of vine ends loose. You will finish appliquéing these ends after the border is attached.

3. Refer to **Border Diagrams** to fuse **flowers (A-D)**, **birds (E)**, and **leaves (H)** in place. Some leaves are near the border seams. Do not fuse these at this time. You will finish stitching those leaves after the border is attached.

4. Refer to **Satin Stitch Appliqué**, page 85, to stitch appliqués in place.

Fig. 1

Triangle-Squares
(make 48)

Block
(make 24)

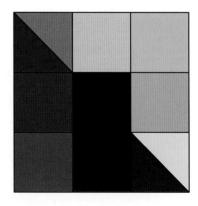

ASSEMBLING THE QUILT TOP

1. Matching centers and corners, sew **side borders** to quilt top center.
2. Matching centers and corners, sew **top** and **bottom borders** to quilt top center.
3. Stitch ends of vines to borders. Add **corner leaves** (F), **flowers** (G), and remaining **leaves** (H) to each of the corners.

COMPLETING THE QUILT

1. Follow **Quilting**, page 89, to mark, layer, and quilt as desired. Quilt shown is machine quilted in a diagonal grid. The border is outline quilted around the appliqués and the background is stipple quilted.
2. Sew **binding strips** together using a diagonal seam (**Fig. 2**) to make a continuous binding strip.
3. Follow **Attaching Binding With Mitered Corners**, page 93, to attach binding.

Side Border Diagram

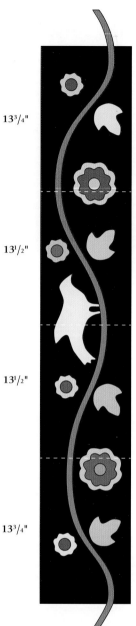

Fig. 2

Top/Bottom Border Diagram

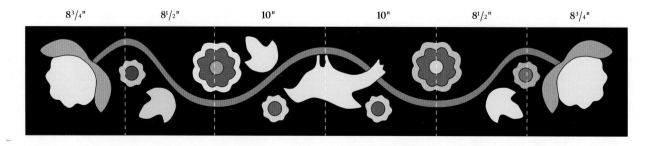

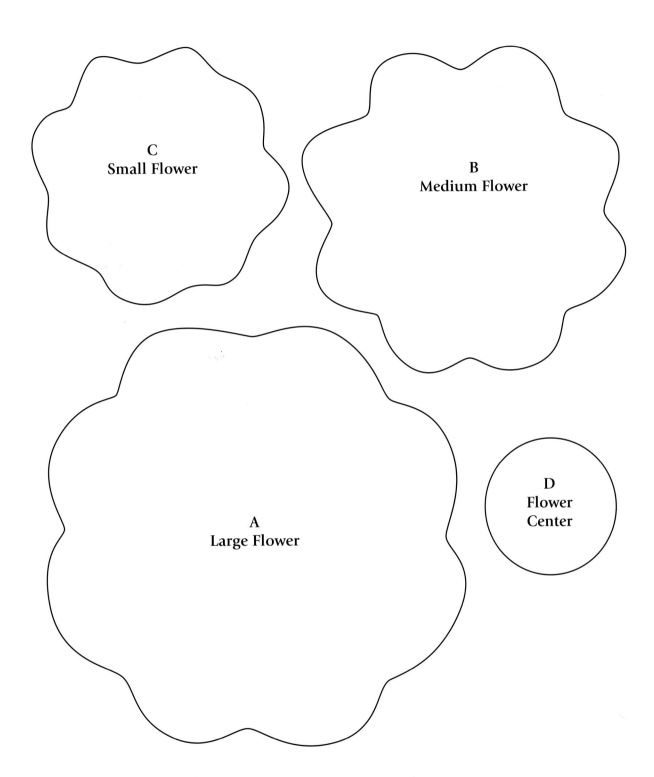

C
Small Flower

B
Medium Flower

A
Large Flower

D
Flower
Center

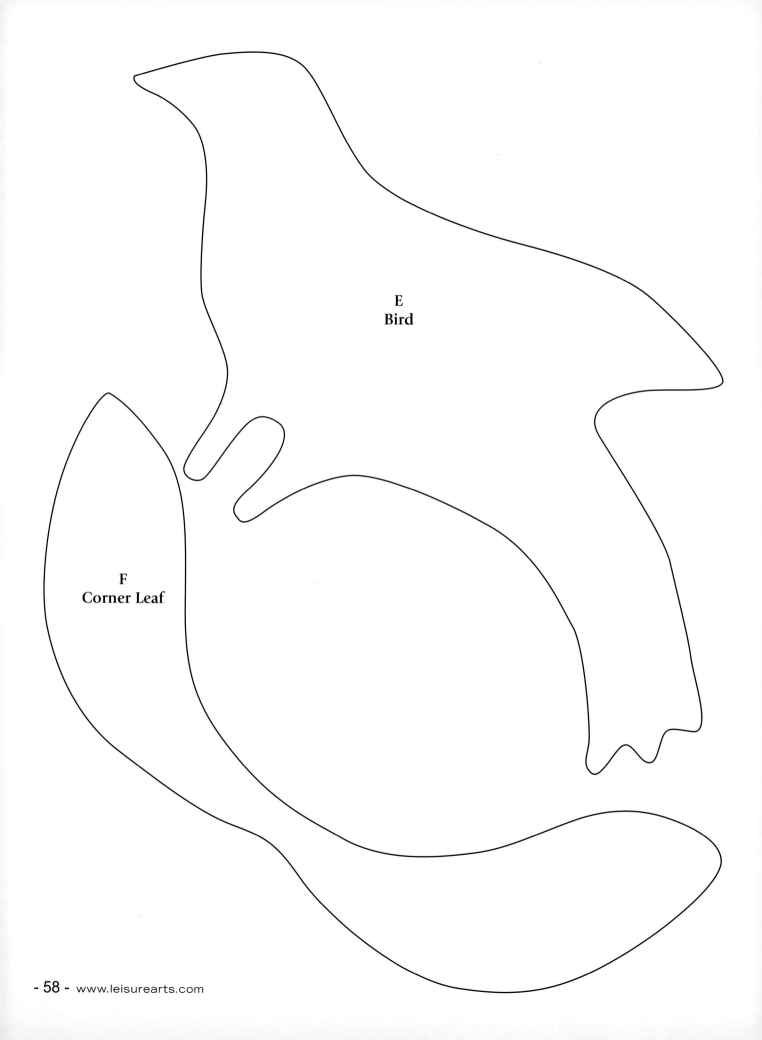

E
Bird

F
Corner Leaf

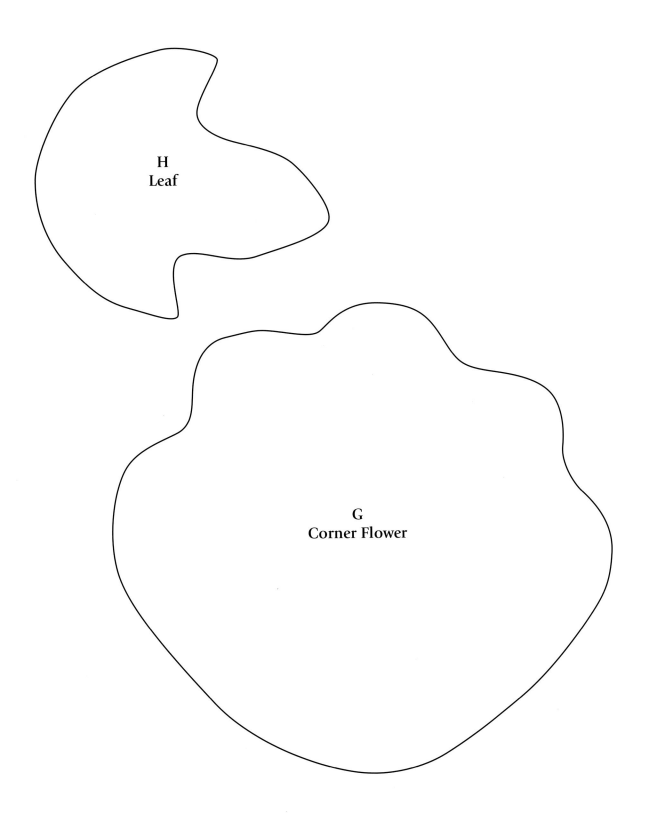

H
Leaf

G
Corner Flower

PINEAPPLES

Finished Table Runner Size: 19" x 65" (48 cm x 165 cm)
Finished Block Size: 16" x 16" (41 cm x 41 cm)

The length of this table runner is easy to adjust by adding or subtracting rows of 4^1/$_2$" squares in the pieced center.

YARDAGE REQUIREMENTS

Yardage is based on 43"/44" (109 cm/112 cm) wide fabric with a usable width of 40" (102 cm).

^{7}/$_8$ yd (80 cm) of cream print fabric for background
^{1}/$_4$ yd (23 cm) of brown #1 print fabric for blocks and squares
12" x 20" (30 cm x 51 cm) piece of brown #2 print fabric for squares
12" x 20" (30 cm x 51 cm) piece of rust print fabric for circles and squares
^{3}/$_8$ yd (34 cm) of gold print fabric for pineapples and squares
^{3}/$_8$ yd (34 cm) of green print fabric for crowns, bases, and squares
^{3}/$_8$ yd (34 cm) of multi-color print fabric for binding
2^1/$_8$ yds (1.9 m) of fabric for backing

You will also need:

27" x 73" (69 cm x 185 cm) piece of batting
Paper-backed fusible web

CUTTING THE PIECES

*Follow **Rotary Cutting**, page 81, to cut fabric. Cut all strips across the selvage to selvage width of the fabric. All measurements include ^{1}/$_4$" seam allowances.*

From cream print fabric:
- Cut 2 strips 9^1/$_2$"w. From these strips, cut 8 **background squares** 9^1/$_2$" x 9^1/$_2$".
- Cut 2 **borders** 1^1/$_2$" x 64^1/$_2$", pieced as needed.

From brown #1 print fabric:
- Cut 1 strip 3"w. From this strip, cut 8 **small squares** 3" x 3".
- Cut 1 strip 4^1/$_2$"w. From this strip, cut 6 **large squares** 4^1/$_2$" x 4^1/$_2$".

From brown #2 print fabric:
- Cut 2 strips 4^1/$_2$" x 20". From these strips, cut 7 **large squares** 4^1/$_2$" x 4^1/$_2$".

From rust print fabric:
- Cut 2 strips 4^1/$_2$" x 20". From these strips, cut 8 **large squares** 4^1/$_2$" x 4^1/$_2$".

From gold print fabric:
- Cut 1 strip 4^1/$_2$"w. From this strip, cut 5 **large squares** 4^1/$_2$" x 4^1/$_2$".

From green print fabric:
- Cut 1 strip 4^1/$_2$"w. From this strip, cut 6 **large squares** 4^1/$_2$" x 4^1/$_2$".

From multi-color print fabric:
- Cut 5 **binding strips** 2^1/$_4$" wide.

CUTTING THE APPLIQUÉS

*Refer to **Preparing Fusible Appliqués**, page 85, and use patterns, page 63, to prepare appliqués.*

From rust print fabric:
- Cut 8 **circles**.

From gold print fabric:
- Cut 8 **pineapples**.

From green print fabric:
- Cut 8 **bases**.
- Cut 8 **crowns**.

ASSEMBLING THE PINEAPPLE BLOCKS

Follow Machine Piecing, page 82, and Pressing, page 83, and use a ¼" seam allowance.

1. Draw a diagonal line on wrong side of each brown #1 print **small square**. With right sides together, place 1 brown #1 print small square in 1 corner of 1 **background square**. Stitch on drawn line (**Fig. 1**).
2. Trim ¼" from stitching line and press brown #1 fabric to right side to make **Unit 1**. Make 8 Unit 1's.
3. Fuse 1 **base**, 1 **crown**, and 1 **pineapple** to 1 Unit 1.
4. Refer to **Satin Stitch Appliqué**, page 85, to stitch appliqués in place to make 1 Unit 2.
5. Repeat Steps 3 and 4 to make a total of 8 Unit 2's. Trim each Unit 2 to 8½" x 8½".
6. Sew 4 Unit 2's together to make **Pineapple Block**. Make 2 Pineapple Blocks.
7. Fuse **circles** to Pineapple Blocks. Stitch appliqués in place in same manner as previous.

ASSEMBLING THE TABLE RUNNER

Refer to Table Runner Top Diagram for assembly.

1. Sew 4 assorted **large squares** together to make a **Row**; press seam allowances in 1 direction. Make 8 Rows.
2. Alternating the direction of the seam allowances, sew Rows together to make quilt top center.
3. Sew 1 Pineapple Block to each end of the quilt top center; press seam allowances toward the center.
4. Sew 1 **border** to each long edge of table runner; press seam allowances toward the borders.

COMPLETING THE TABLE RUNNER

1. Follow **Quilting**, page 89, to mark, layer, and quilt as desired. Quilt shown is machine quilted with a diagonal crosshatch grid in the quilt top center and each pineapple and stipple quilting in the background of the Pineapple Blocks. The appliqués are stitched in the ditch. There are curlicue tendrils stitched around the pineapples. The center triangles of each block are quilted through the center.

2. Sew **binding strips** together using a diagonal seam (**Fig. 2**) to make a continuous binding strip.
3. Follow **Attaching Binding With Mitered Corners**, page 93, to attach binding.

Fig. 1

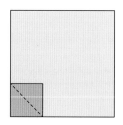

Unit 1 (make 8)

Unit 2

Pineapple Block (make 2)

Fig. 2

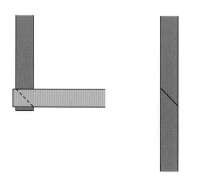

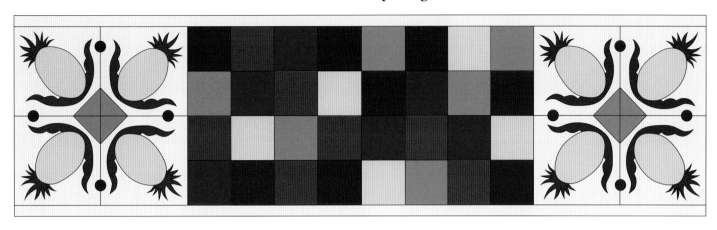

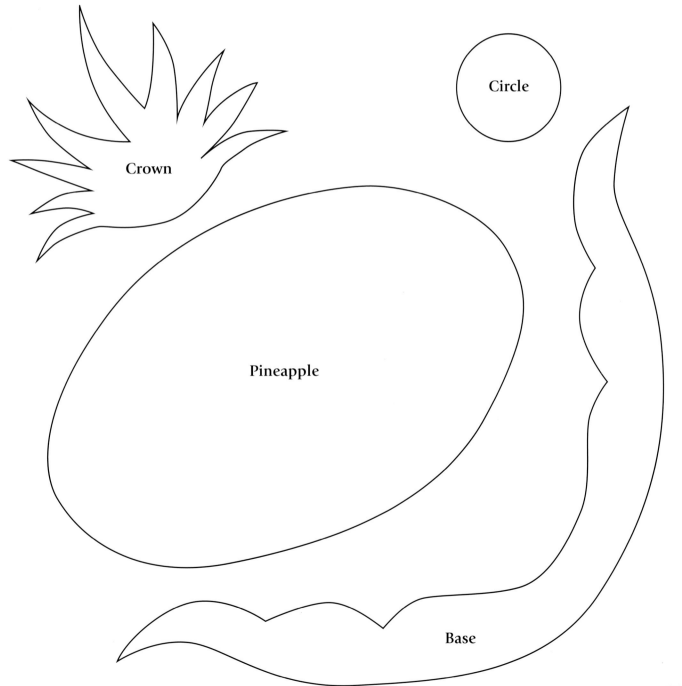

Crown

Circle

Pineapple

Base

WINTER GARDEN

Finished Quilt Size: 88" x 88" (224 cm x 224 cm)
Finished Block Size: 7¹/₂" x 7¹/₂" (19 cm x 19 cm)

YARDAGE REQUIREMENTS

Yardage is based on 43"/44" (109 cm/112 cm) wide fabric with a usable width of 40" (102 cm).

- ¹/₄ yd (23 cm) of gold print fabric
- 3⁷/₈ yds (3.5 m) of black print fabric
- 3⁵/₈ yds (3.3 m) *total* of assorted light print (yellow, gold, and cream) fabrics
- 3³/₈ yds (3.1 m) *total* of assorted grey print fabrics
- 8 yds (7.3 m) of fabric for backing

You will also need:

- 96" x 96" (244 cm x 244 cm) piece of batting

CUTTING THE PIECES

*Follow **Rotary Cutting**, page 81, to cut fabric. Cut all strips across the selvage-to-selvage width of the fabric. Borders include extra length for "insurance" and will be trimmed after assembling quilt top center. All measurements include ¹/₄" seam allowances.*

From gold print fabric:

- Cut 3 strips 2"w. From these strips, cut 60 **sashing squares** 2" x 2".

From black print fabric:

- Cut 5 strips 8"w. From these strips, cut 100 **sashing strips** 2" x 8".
- Cut 2 *lengthwise* **side outer borders** 2" x 88¹/₂".
- Cut 2 *lengthwise* **top/bottom outer borders** 2" x 91¹/₂".
- Cut 2 *lengthwise* **side middle borders** 2" x 79¹/₂".
- Cut 2 *lengthwise* **top/bottom middle borders** 2" x 82¹/₂".
- Cut 2 *lengthwise* **side inner borders** 2¹/₈" x 70¹/₄".
- Cut 2 *lengthwise* **top/bottom inner borders** 2¹/₈" x 73¹/₂".
- Cut 4 *lengthwise* **binding strips** 2¹/₂" x 95¹/₂".

From assorted light print fabrics:

- Cut 41 sets of 4 **squares (A)** 3" x 3" and 2 **squares (B)** 3¹/₂" x 3¹/₂". Cut each set from 1 fabric.
- Cut 46 squares 4¹/₄" x 4¹/₄". Cut each square *twice* diagonally to make 184 **triangles (H)**.
- Cut 8 squares 2³/₈" x 2³/₈". Cut each square *once* diagonally to make 16 **triangles (I)**.
- Cut 54 **squares (J)** 4" x 4".

From assorted grey print fabrics:

- Cut 41 sets of 1 **square (A)** 3" x 3" and 2 **squares (B)** 3¹/₂" x 3¹/₂". Cut each set from 1 fabric.
- Cut 4 squares 14" x 14". Cut each square *twice* diagonally to make 16 **side setting triangles (E)**. *(**Note:** More fabrics can be used for more variety if desired but you will have triangles left over.)*
- Cut 2 squares 8³/₈" x 8³/₈". Cut each square *once* diagonally to make 4 **corner setting triangles (F)**.
- Cut 96 **squares (G)** 2⁵/₈" x 2⁵/₈".
- Cut 54 **squares (J)** 4" x 4".

ASSEMBLING THE BLOCKS

Follow Machine Piecing, page 82, and Pressing, page 83. Use a $^1/_4$" seam allowance for piecing.

1. For each block, choose 1 set of 2 grey **squares** (**B**) and 1 grey **square** (**A**). Choose 1 set of 2 light **squares** (**B**) and 4 light **squares** (**A**).
2. Draw a diagonal line on wrong side of each light square (**B**). With right sides together, place 1 light square (**B**) on top of 1 grey square (**B**). Stitch seam $^1/_4$" from each side of drawn line (**Fig. 1**).
3. Cut along drawn line and press seam allowances toward the grey triangle to make 2 **Triangle-Square A's**. Make 4 Triangle-Square A's. Trim each Triangle-Square A to 3" x 3".
4. Sew 2 Triangle-Squares and 1 light square (A) together to make **Row 1**. Make 2 Row 1's.
5. Sew 2 light squares (A) and 1 grey square (A) together to make **Row 2**.
6. Sew Row 1's and Row 2 together to make Block. Repeat Steps 1-6 to make a total of 41 Blocks.

ASSEMBLING THE QUILT TOP CENTER

1. Refer to **Assembly Diagram**, page 69, to lay out **Blocks**, **sashing strips**, **sashing squares**, **side setting triangles** (**E**), and **corner setting triangles** (**F**).
2. Sew pieces together in diagonal rows. Add corner setting triangles to each corner.
3. Trim edges of quilt $^1/_4$" from points of sashings squares. Quilt top should measure approximately $66^1/_4$" x $66^1/_4$".

ADDING THE BORDERS

Inner Border
1. Refer to **Adding Squared Borders**, page 88, to add **side inner borders**, then **top** and **bottom inner borders** to quilt top.

Inner Pieced Border
*Refer to **Border Diagrams**, page 68, for placement.*
1. Sew 1 **square (G)**, 1 **triangle (H)**, and 2 **triangles (I)** together to make **Corner Border Unit**. Make 8 Corner Border Units.
2. Sew 1 **square (G)** and 2 **triangles (H)** together to make **Border Unit**. Make 88 Border Units.
3. Sew 21 Border Units and 2 Corner Border Units together to make **Side Inner Pieced Border**. Make 2 **Side Inner Pieced Borders**.
4. Sew 23 Border Units and 2 Corner Border Units together to make **Top Inner Pieced Border**. Repeat to make **Bottom Inner Pieced Border**.
5. Sew Side Inner Pieced Borders to quilt top center. Press seam allowances toward the black Inner Border.
6. Sew Top and Bottom Inner Pieced Borders to quilt top center. Press seam allowances toward the black inner border.

Middle Border
1. Add **Middle Borders** to quilt top in same manner as Inner Borders.

Outer Pieced Border
1. Draw a diagonal line on wrong side of each light **square (J)**. With right sides together, place 1 light square (J) on top of 1 grey **square (J)**. Stitch seam $1/4$" from each side of drawn line (**Fig. 2**).
2. Cut along drawn line and press seam allowances toward the grey triangle to make 2 **Triangle-Square B's**. Make 108 Triangle-Square B's. Trim all Triangle-Square B's to $3^1/_2$" x $3^1/_2$".

Fig. 1

Triangle-Square A's (make 4)

Row 1 (make 2)

Row 2

Block (make 41)

Corner Border Unit (make 8)

Border Unit (make 88)

Fig. 2

Triangle-Square B's (make 108)

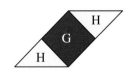

3. Sew 26 Triangle-Square B's together, reversing the direction of the triangles in the center to make **Side Outer Pieced Border**. Make 2 **Side Outer Pieced Borders**.

4. Sew 28 Triangle-Square B's together, reversing the direction of the triangles in the center and at the ends to make **Top Outer Pieced Border**. Repeat to make **Bottom Outer Pieced Border**.

5. Sew Side Outer Pieced Borders to quilt top. Sew Top/Bottom Outer Pieced Borders to the quilt top.

Outer Border

1. Add **Outer Borders** to quilt top in same manner as Inner and Middle Borders.

Side Inner Pieced Border (make 2)

Top/Bottom Inner Pieced Border (make 2)

Side Outer Pieced Border (make 2)

Top/Bottom Outer Pieced Border (make 2)

FINISHING THE QUILT

1. Follow **Quilting**, page 89, to mark, layer, and quilt. Our quilt is machine quilted with a feather motif in each block. All borders, sashings, and Triangle-Squares in borders are stitched in the ditch.
2. Sew **binding strips** together using a diagonal seam (**Fig. 3**) to make a continuous binding strip.
3. Follow **Attaching Binding with Mitered Corners**, page 93, to attach binding.

Fig. 3

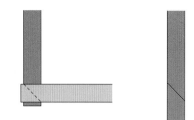

Assembly Diagram

COUNTRY CROSSROADS

Finished Quilt Size: 78³/₄" x 78³/₄" (200 cm x 200 cm)
Finished Block Size: 8" x 8" (20 cm x 20 cm)

YARDAGE REQUIREMENTS

Yardage is based on 43"/44" (109 cm/112 cm) wide fabric with a usable width of 40" (102 cm).

  1 yd (91 cm) of cream print fabric
  1¹/₈ yds (1 m) of grey print fabric
  2³/₈ yds (2.2 m) of tan floral print fabric
  3¹/₂ yds (3.2 m) of burgundy print fabric
  ³/₄ yd (69 cm) of light green print fabric
  ⁵/₈ yd (57 cm) of medium green print fabric
  ³/₄ yd (69 cm) of dark green print fabric
  ³/₄ yd (69 cm) *total* of assorted light print fabrics
  1¹/₄ yds (1.1 m) *total* of assorted medium and dark print fabrics
  ³/₈ yd (34 cm) *total* of assorted pink and red print fabrics
  7¹/₄ yds (6.6 m) of fabric for backing

You will also need:

  87" x 87" (221 cm x 221 cm) piece of batting
  That Patchwork Place® 8¹/₂" x 11"
    (22 cm x 28 cm) papers for foundation piecing
  Optional: ³/₄" (19 mm) bias pressing bar

CUTTING THE PIECES

Follow Rotary Cutting, page 81, to cut fabric. Cut all strips across the selvage-to-selvage width of the fabric. Borders include extra length for "insurance" and will be trimmed after assembling quilt top center. All measurements include ¹/₄" seam allowances. Use patterns, pages 78-79, and follow Making and Using Templates, page 84, to make 1 appliqué template for each pattern.

From cream print fabric:
- Cut 3 strips 8¹/₂"w. From these strips, cut 12 **squares** (A) 8¹/₂" x 8¹/₂".
- Cut 1 strip 7"w. From this strip, cut 2 **squares** (C) 7" x 7".

From grey print fabric:
- Cut 4 strips 8¹/₂"w. From these strips, cut 8 **rectangles** (B) 8¹/₂" x 16¹/₂".

From tan floral print fabric:
- Cut 2 *lengthwise* **side outer borders** 4" x 82¹/₄".
- Cut 2 *lengthwise* **top/bottom outer borders** 4" x 75¹/₄".

From remaining width:
- Cut 4 strips 7"w. From these strips, cut 10 **squares** (C) 7" x 7".
- Cut 20 strips 2¹/₄"w. From these strips, cut 196 **squares** (G) 2¹/₄" x 2¹/₄".
- Cut 1 strip 1¹/₂"w. From this strip, cut 8 **rectangles** (H) 1¹/₂" x 2¹/₂".

From burgundy print fabric:
- Cut 1 **square** (A) 8¹/₂" x 8¹/₂".
- Cut 3 strips 7"w. From this strip, cut 12 **squares** (C) 7" x 7".
- Cut 2 strips 12⁵/₈"w. From these strips, cut 5 squares 12⁵/₈" x 12⁵/₈". Cut each square *twice* diagonally to make 20 **side setting triangles** (E).
- Cut 1 strip 6⁵/₈"w. From this strip, cut 2 squares 6⁵/₈" x 6⁵/₈". Cut each square *once* diagonally to make 4 **corner setting triangles** (F).
- Cut 12 strips 2¹/₄"w. From these strips, cut 192 **squares** (G) 2¹/₄" x 2¹/₄".
- Cut 9 **binding strips** 2¹/₂" wide.

From light green print fabric:
- Use template to cut 52 **leaves**.
- Use template to cut 4 **flower part #6's**.

From medium green print fabric:
- Cut a 19" x 19" square. Refer to **Making A Continuous Bias Strip**, page 92, to cut a 2"w bias strip. Cut bias strip into 8 **vines** 2" x 18".
- Use template to cut 20 **leaves**.

Continued on page 72.

From dark green print fabric:
- Use template to cut 32 **leaves**.
- Use template to cut 4 **flower part #3's**.
- Use template to cut 4 **flower part #3's** in reverse.

From assorted light print fabrics:
- Cut 84 **squares (D)** 3" x 3".

From assorted medium and dark print fabrics:
- Cut 8 **squares (A)** $8^1/_2$" x $8^1/_2$".
- Cut 60 **squares (D)** 3" x 3".
- Use template to cut 4 **flower part #1's**.
- Use template to cut 4 **flower part #2's**.
- Use template to cut 4 **flower part #5's**.

From assorted pink and red print fabrics:
- Cut 24 **squares (D)** 3" x 3".
- Use template to cut 4 **flower part #1's**.
- Use template to cut 4 **flower part #2's**.
- Use template to cut 4 **flower part #4's**.

MAKING THE BLOCKS

Follow **Machine Piecing**, *page 82, and* **Pressing**, *page 83. Use a $^1/_4$" seam allowance for piecing.*

1. Draw a diagonal line on the wrong side of 1 light print **square (D)**. Matching right sides, place light print square (D) on top of 1 medium/dark print **square (D)**. Stitch $^1/_4$" from each side of drawn line (**Fig. 1**). Cut along drawn line; press open, pressing seam allowances toward the darker fabric to make 2 **Unit 1's**. Using remaining medium/dark print squares (D), pink/red print squares (D), and light print squares (D), make a total of 168 Unit 1's. Trim each Unit 1 to $2^1/_2$" x $2^1/_2$".

2. Repeat Step 1 using burgundy **squares (C)** and cream print **squares (C)** to make 4 **Unit 2's**. Trim each Unit 2 to $6^1/_2$" x $6^1/_2$".

3. Repeat Step 1 using burgundy **squares (C)** and tan floral print **squares (C)** to make 20 **Unit 3's**. Trim each Unit 3 to $6^1/_2$" x $6^1/_2$".

4. Sew 3 Unit 1's together to make **Unit 4**. Make 24 Unit 4's.

5. Sew 4 Unit 1's together to make **Unit 5**. Make 24 Unit 5's.

6. Sew 1 Unit 4 to 1 side of Unit 2. Sew 1 Unit 5 to the adjacent side of Unit 2 to make **Block A**. Make 4 Block A's.

7. Sew 1 Unit 4 to 1 side of Unit 3. Sew 1 Unit 5 to the adjacent side of Unit 3 to make **Block B**. Make 20 Block B's.

Fig. 1

Unit 1 (make 168)

Unit 2 (make 4)

Unit 3 (make 20)

Unit 4 (make 24)

Unit 5 (make 24)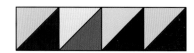

Block A (make 4)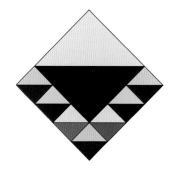

Block B (make 20)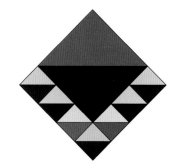

ASSEMBLING THE APPLIQUÉ BLOCKS

1. Sew 1 Block A and 3 cream **squares (A)** together to make 1 **Unit 6**. Make 4 Unit 6's.
2. Refer to **Needle-Turn Appliqué**, page 84, to stitch flower pieces 1-6 and leaves in place on Unit 6 to make **Flower Block**. In order to tuck the stems under the burgundy triangle, take out part of the seam, insert the stems, and re-sew the seam. Repeat to make a total of 4 Flower Blocks.
3. Matching wrong sides, fold each **bias strip** for vine in half lengthwise. Stitch 1/4" from raw edges. Centering seam allowance on back, press tube flat. Trim seam allowance if necessary. Using a 3/4" bias pressing bar makes pressing faster and easier.
4. Position 1 vine and 12 leaves on each **rectangle (B)** and stitch in place to make **Vine Block** in same manner as Flower Block. Make 8 Vine Blocks.

Unit 6 (make 4)

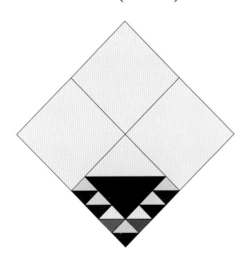

Flower Block (make 4)

ASSEMBLING THE QUILT TOP CENTER

*Refer to **Assembly Diagram**, page 75.*

1. Sew 2 Flower Blocks and 1 Vine Block together to make **Row 1**. Make 2 Row 1's.
2. Sew 2 Vine Blocks and 1 burgundy **square (A)** together to make **Row 2**.

Vine Block (make 8)

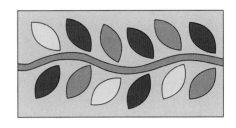

Row 1 (make 2)

Row 2

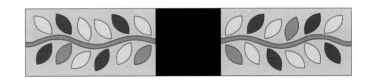

3. Sew Row 1's and Row 2 together to make **Unit 7**.
4. Sew 2 **side setting triangles** (**E**) and 1 medium/dark print **square** (**A**) together to make **Unit 8**. Make 8 Unit 8's.
5. Sew 2 Unit 8's, 1 Vine Block, and 1 **corner setting triangle** (**F**) together to make **Unit 9**. Make 4 Unit 9's.
6. Sew 5 Block B's together to make **Unit 10**. Make 2 Unit 10's.
7. Sew 5 Block B's together to make **Unit 11**. Make 2 Unit 11's.
8. Sew 1 side setting triangle (**E**) to each end of 1 Unit 10 to make **Unit 12**. Make 2 Unit 12's.

Unit 9 (make 4)

Unit 7

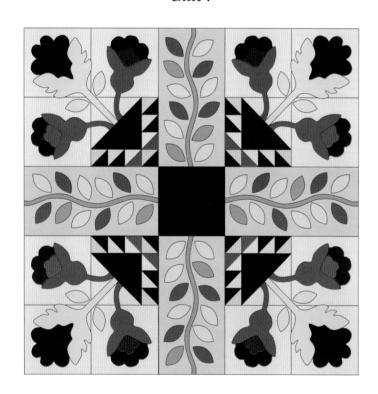

Unit 10 (make 2)

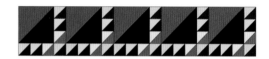

Unit 11 (make 2)

Unit 12 (make 2)

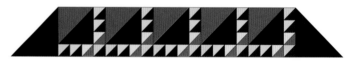

Unit 8 (make 8)

9. Sew 1 Unit 9 and 1 Unit 11 together to make **Unit 13**. Make 2 Unit 13's.
10. Sew 1 Unit 9 and 1 Unit 12 together to make **Unit 14**. Make 2 Unit 14's.
11. Sew 1 Unit 13 to opposite sides of Unit 7. Sew 1 Unit 14 to each remaining side to complete quilt top center.

ADDING THE BORDERS

1. Make 2 photocopies of Top/Bottom End Unit 1, 2 photocopies of Top/Bottom End Unit 2, 2 photocopies of Side End Unit 1, 2 photocopies of Side End Unit 2, and 44 photocopies of the Center Unit pattern, onto foundation piecing paper.
2. Refer to **Foundation Paper Piecing**, page 83, to make border units. Using **rectangles (H)** for small triangles and alternating tan floral and burgundy **squares (G)** for large triangles and working in numerical order, paper piece 2 each of Top/Bottom End Unit 1, Top/Bottom End Unit 2, Side End Unit 1, Side End Unit 2, and 44 of Center Unit.
3. **Do not** remove paper foundations. Trim Units along outer line on pattern.
4. Sew 11 of the paper pieced Center Units together. Sew 1 Top/Bottom End Unit 1 to 1 end of Center Units. Sew 1 Top/Bottom End Unit 2 to remaining end of Center Units to make 1 **Top Inner Border**. Repeat to make **Bottom Inner Border**.
5. Sew 11 of the paper pieced Center Units together. Sew 1 Side End Unit 1 to 1 end of Center Units. Sew 1 Side End Unit 2 to remaining end of Center Units to make 1 **Side Inner Border**. Make 2 **Side Inner Borders**.
6. Matching centers and corners, sew Top and Bottom Inner Pieced Borders to quilt top. Sew Side Inner Pieced Borders to quilt top. Remove paper.
7. Refer to **Adding Squared Borders**, page 88, to add **top**, **bottom**, and then **side outer borders** to quilt top.

Unit 13 (make 2)

Unit 14 (make 2)

Side End Unit 1

Side End Unit 2

Center Unit

Top/Bottom End Unit 1

Top/Bottom End Unit 2

Top/Bottom End Unit 1

Top/Bottom End Unit 2

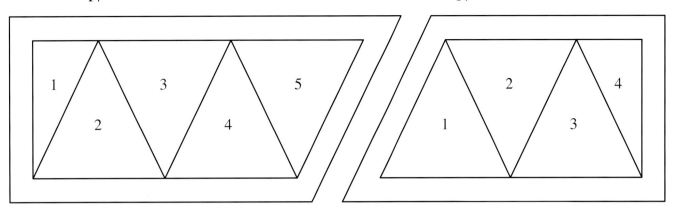

Side End Unit 1

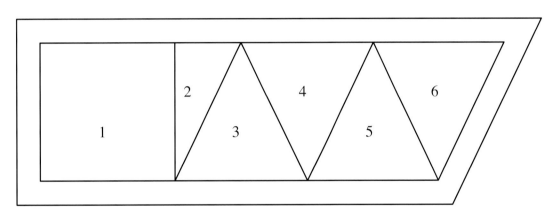

Side End Unit 2

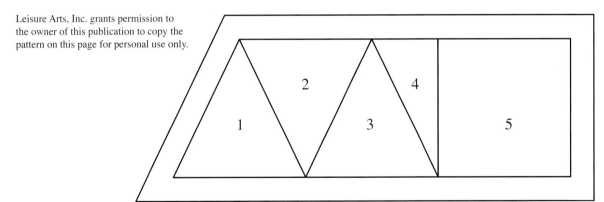

Center Unit

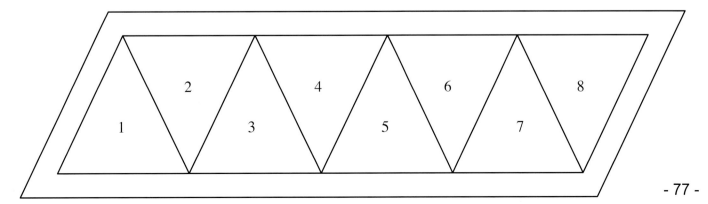

FINISHING THE QUILT

1. Follow **Quilting**, page 89, to mark, layer, and quilt. Our quilt is machine quilted.
2. Sew **binding strips** together using a diagonal seam (**Fig. 2**) to make a continuous binding strip.
3. Follow **Attaching Binding with Mitered Corners**, page 93, to attach binding.

Fig. 2

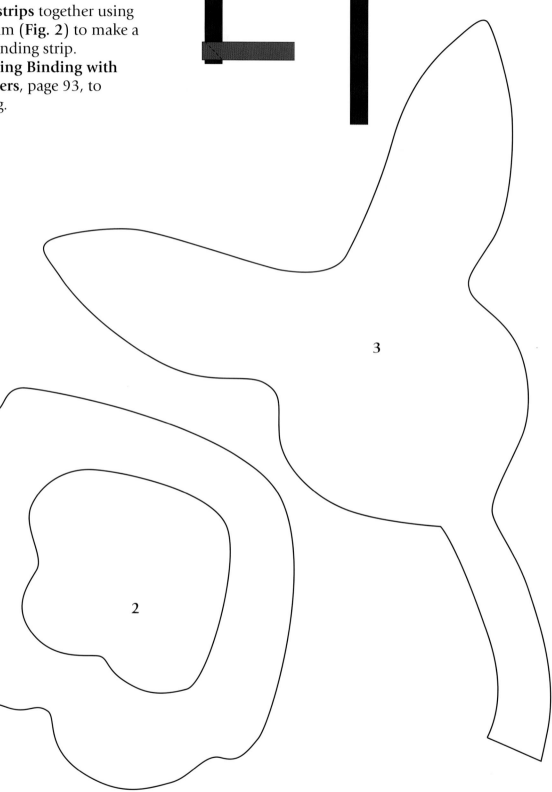

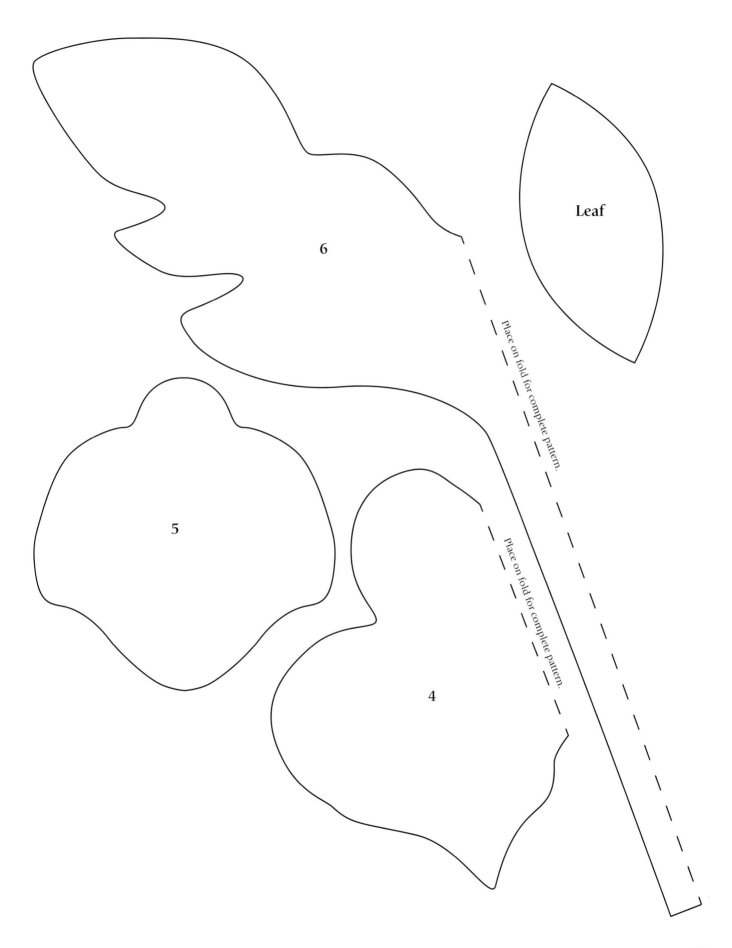

Leaf

6

5

4

Place on fold for complete pattern.

Place on fold for complete pattern.

GENERAL INSTRUCTIONS

To make your quilting easier and more enjoyable, we encourage you to carefully read all of the general instructions, study the color photographs, and familiarize yourself with the individual project instructions before beginning a project.

FABRICS
SELECTING FABRICS
Choose high-quality, medium-weight 100% cotton fabrics. All-cotton fabrics hold a crease better, fray less, and are easier to quilt than cotton/polyester blends.

Yardage requirements listed for each project are based on 43"/44" wide fabric with a "usable" width of 40" after shrinkage and trimming selvages. Actual usable width will probably vary slightly from fabric to fabric. Our recommended yardage lengths should be adequate for occasional re-squaring of fabric when many cuts are required.

PREPARING FABRICS
Pre-washing fabrics may cause edges to ravel. As a result, your pre-cut fabric pieces may not be large enough to cut all of the pieces required for your chosen project. Therefore, we do not recommend pre-washing your yardage or pre-cut fabrics.

Before cutting, prepare fabrics with a steam iron set on cotton and starch or sizing. The starch or sizing will give the fabric a crisp finish. This will make cutting more accurate and may make piecing easier.

ROTARY CUTTING
CUTTING FROM YARDAGE

- Place fabric on work surface with fold closest to you.
- Cut all strips from the selvage-to-selvage width of the fabric.
- Square left edge of fabric using rotary cutter and rulers (**Figs. 1 - 2**).
- To cut each strip required for a project, place ruler over cut edge of fabric, aligning desired marking on ruler with cut edge; make cut (**Fig. 3**).
- When cutting several strips from a single piece of fabric, it is important to make sure that cuts remain at a perfect right angle to the fold; square fabric as needed.

CUTTING FROM FAT QUARTERS OR FAT EIGHTHS

- Place fabric flat on work surface with lengthwise (short) edge closest to you.
- Cut all strips parallel to the long edge of the fabric in the same manner as cutting from yardage.
- To cut each strip required for a project, place ruler over cut edge of fabric, aligning desired marking on ruler with cut edge; make cut.

Fig. 1

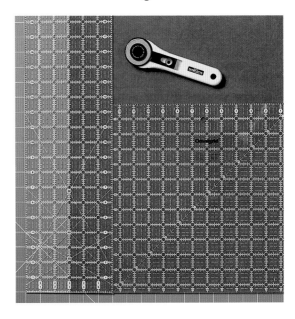

Fig. 2

Fig. 3

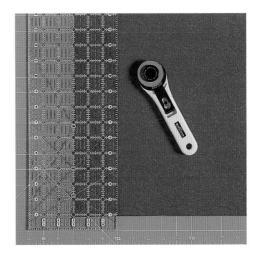

MACHINE PIECING

Precise cutting, followed by accurate piecing, will ensure that all pieces of quilt top fit together well.

- Set sewing machine stitch length for approximately 11 stitches per inch.
- Use neutral-colored general-purpose sewing thread (not quilting thread) in needle and in bobbin.
- An accurate $1/4$" seam allowance is *essential*. Presser feet that are $1/4$" wide are available for most sewing machines.
- When piecing, always place pieces right sides together and match raw edges; pin if necessary.
- Chain piecing saves time and will usually result in more accurate piecing.
- Trim away points of seam allowances that extend beyond edges of sewn pieces.

SEWING STRIP SETS

When there are several strips to assemble into a strip set, first sew strips together into pairs, then sew pairs together to form strip set. To help avoid distortion, sew seams in opposite directions (**Fig. 4**).

SEWING ACROSS SEAM INTERSECTIONS

When sewing across intersection of two seams, place pieces right sides together and match seams exactly, making sure seam allowances are pressed in opposite directions (**Fig. 5**).

SEWING SHARP POINTS

To ensure sharp points when joining triangular or diagonal pieces, stitch across the center of the "X" (shown in pink) formed on wrong side by previous seams (**Fig. 6**).

Fig. 4

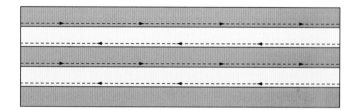

Fig. 5

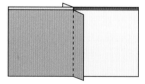

Fig. 6

FOUNDATION PAPER PIECING

1. Projects involving paper piecing will provide a foundation pattern. Photocopy pattern the number of times indicated in the project instructions.
2. Using neutral-colored thread, follow numerical order to place and sew fabrics.
3. With wrong sides together, cover area 1 of foundation with fabric for area 1. Pin fabric in place. Fold foundation on line between area 1 and area 2 (**Fig. 7**). Trim fabric ¼" from fold. Unfold foundation.
4. Matching right sides and trimmed edges, place fabric piece #2 on fabric piece #1 (**Fig. 8**), making sure fabric extends beyond outer edges of area 2. Turn foundation over to front and pin.
5. Sew along line between areas 1 and 2, extending sewing a few stitches beyond beginning and end of line (**Fig. 9**).
6. Open out piece #2; press. Pin piece #2 to foundation (**Fig. 10**).
7. Continue adding pieces in same manner in numerical order until foundation is covered.
8. Trim fabric and foundation along outer lines to complete block. Carefully remove paper foundation.

PRESSING

- Use steam iron set on "Cotton" for all pressing.
- Press after sewing each seam.
- Seam allowances are almost always pressed to one side, usually toward darker fabric. However, to reduce bulk it may occasionally be necessary to press seam allowances toward the lighter fabric or even to press them open.
- To prevent dark fabric seam allowance from showing through light fabric, trim darker seam allowance slightly narrower than lighter seam allowance.
- To press long seams, such as those in long strip sets, without curving or other distortion, lay strips across width of the ironing board.

Fig. 7

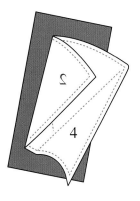

Fig. 9

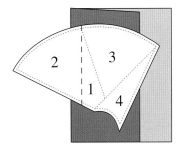

Fig. 8

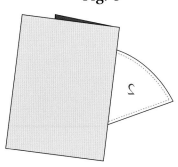

Fig. 10

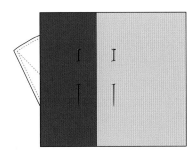

MAKING AND USING TEMPLATES

Piecing template patterns have 2 lines — a solid cutting line and a dashed line showing the ¹/₄" seam allowance. Appliqué template patterns do not include seam allowances.

1. To make a template from a pattern, use a permanent fine-point pen to carefully trace pattern onto template plastic, making sure to transfer any alignment and grainline markings. Cut out template along inner edge of drawn line. Check template against original pattern for accuracy.

2. If using an appliqué template, place template on **right** side of appliqué fabric. Lightly draw around template with pencil, leaving at least 1" between shapes. Repeat for number of shapes specified in project instructions. Cut out shapes approximately ³/₁₆" outside drawn line. Clip inside curves and points to but not through drawn line.

3. If using a piecing template, use a sharp fabric-marking pencil to draw around template on **wrong** side of fabric, aligning grainline on template with straight grain of fabric. Repeat for number of pieces specified in project instructions. Cut out fabric piece using scissors or rotary cutting equipment.

NEEDLE-TURN APPLIQUÉ

Patterns for Needle-Turn Appliqué do not include seam allowances. Using your needle to turn under the seam allowance while blindstitching (page 95) an appliqué piece to the background fabric is called "needle-turn" appliqué.

1. Thread a sharps needle with a single strand of general-purpose sewing thread that matches appliqué; knot one end.

2. Begin blindstitching on as straight an edge as possible, turning a small section of ³/₁₆" seam allowance to wrong side with needle, concealing drawn line (**Fig. 11**). Clip curves as needed, up to but not through drawn line.

3. To stitch outward points, stitch to ¹/₂" from point (**Fig. 12**). Turn seam allowance under at point (**Fig. 13**); then turn remainder of seam allowance between stitching and point. Stitch to point, taking two or three stitches at top of point to secure. Turn under small amount of seam allowance past point and resume stitching.

4. To stitch inward point, stitch to ¹/₂" from point (**Fig. 14**). Clip to but not through seam allowance at point (**Fig. 15**). Turn seam allowance under between stitching and point. Stitch to point, taking two or three stitches at point to secure. Turn under small amount of seam allowance past point and resume stitching.

Fig. 11   **Fig. 12**

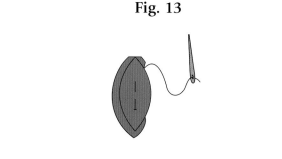

Fig. 13

Fig. 14   **Fig. 15**

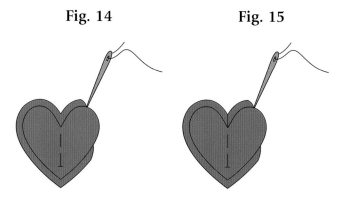

5. Do not turn under or stitch seam allowances that will be covered by other appliqué pieces.

6. For appliqué pieces that are layered (such as a flower center on top of a flower), appliqué top piece to bottom piece before appliquéing bottom piece to background.

7. To appliqué pressed bias strips, baste strips in place and blindstitch along edges.

8. To reduce bulk, background fabric behind appliqués may be cut away. After stitching appliqués in place, turn background over and use sharp scissors or specially designed appliqué scissors to trim away background fabric approximately $1/4$" from stitching line. Take care not to cut appliqué fabric or stitches. Bulk may be reduced behind layered appliqués by cutting away bottom layer of appliqués.

MACHINE APPLIQUÉ
PREPARING FUSIBLE APPLIQUÉS
White or light-colored fabrics may need to be lined with fusible interfacing before applying fusible web to prevent darker fabrics from showing through.

1. Place paper-backed fusible web, paper side up, over appliqué pattern. Trace pattern onto paper side of web with pencil as many times as indicated in project instructions for a single fabric.

2. Follow manufacturer's instructions to fuse traced patterns to wrong side of fabrics. Do not remove paper backing.

3. Use scissors to cut out appliqué pieces along traced lines. Remove paper backing from all pieces.

PREPARING BLANKET STITCH OR ZIGZAG STITCH APPLIQUÉS

1. Center template on **wrong** side of appliqué fabric.

2. Lightly draw around template with a sharp fabric-marking pencil, leaving at least 1" between shapes. Repeat for number of shapes specified in project instructions. Cut out shapes approximately $3/8$" outside drawn line. Clip inside curves to but not through drawn line.

3. Beginning at point (if any) press raw edges of appliqué over edges of template.

SATIN STITCH APPLIQUÉ
A good satin stitch is a thick, smooth, almost solid line of zigzag stitching that covers the exposed raw edges of appliqué pieces.

1. Pin stabilizer, such as paper or any of the commercially available products, on wrong side of background fabric before stitching appliqués in place.

2. Thread sewing machine with general-purpose thread; use general-purpose thread that matches background fabric in bobbin.

3. Set sewing machine for a medium (approximately $1/8$") zigzag stitch and a short stitch length. Slightly loosening the top tension may yield a smoother stitch.

4. Begin by stitching two or three stitches in place (drop feed dogs or set stitch length at 0) to anchor thread. Most of the Satin Stitch should be on the appliqué with the right edge of the stitch falling at the outside edge of the appliqué. Stitch over all exposed raw edges of appliqué pieces.

5. (*Note: Dots on **Figs. 16 – 21** indicate where to leave needle in fabric when pivoting.*) For outside corners, stitch just past corner, stopping with needle in background fabric (**Fig. 16**). Raise presser foot. Pivot project, lower presser foot, and stitch adjacent side (**Fig. 17**).
6. For inside corners, stitch just past corner, stopping with needle in appliqué fabric (**Fig. 18**). Raise presser foot. Pivot project, lower presser foot, and stitch adjacent side (**Fig. 19**).
7. When stitching outside curves, stop with needle in background fabric. Raise presser foot and pivot project as needed. Lower presser foot and continue stitching, pivoting as often as necessary to follow curve (**Fig. 20**).
8. When stitching inside curves, stop with needle in appliqué fabric. Raise presser foot and pivot project as needed. Lower presser foot and continue stitching, pivoting as often as necessary to follow curve (**Fig. 21**).
9. Do not backstitch at end of stitching. Pull threads to wrong side of background fabric; knot thread and trim ends.
10. Carefully tear away stabilizer.

BLANKET STITCH APPLIQUÉ

Some sewing machines are capable of a Blanket Stitch. Refer to your owner's manual for machine set-up. If your machine does not have this stitch, try any of the decorative stitches your machine has until you are satisfied with the look.

1. Thread sewing machine and bobbin with 100% cotton thread in desired weight.
2. Attach an open-toe presser foot. Select far right needle position and needle down (if your machine has these features).
3. If desired, pin a stabilizer, such as paper or any of the commercially available products, on wrong side of background fabric before stitching appliqués in place.
4. Bring bobbin thread to the top of the fabric by lowering then raising the needle, bringing up the bobbin thread loop. Pull the loop all the way to the surface.
5. Begin by stitching two or three stitches in place (drop feed dogs or set stitch length at 0), or use your machine's lock stitch feature, if equipped, to anchor thread. Return setting to selected Blanket Stitch.
6. Most of the Blanket Stitch should be on the appliqué with the right edges of the stitch falling at the very outside edge of the appliqué. Stitch over all exposed raw edges of appliqué pieces.

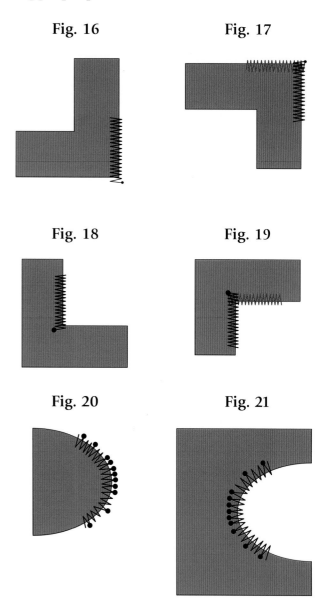

Fig. 16   Fig. 17

Fig. 18   Fig. 19

Fig. 20   Fig. 21

7. (*Note: Dots on Figs. 22 – 26 indicate where to leave needle in fabric when pivoting.*) Always stopping with needle down in background fabric, refer to **Fig. 22** to stitch outside points like tips of leaves. Stop one stitch short of point. Raise presser foot. Pivot project slightly, lower presser foot, and make an angled Stitch 1. Take next stitch, stop at point, and pivot so Stitch 2 will be perpendicular to point. Pivot slightly to make Stitch 3. Continue stitching.

8. For outside corners (**Fig. 23**), stitch to corner, stopping with needle in background fabric. Raise presser foot. Pivot project, lower presser foot, and take an angled stitch. Raise presser foot. Pivot project, lower presser foot and stitch adjacent side.

9. For inside corners (**Fig. 24**), stitch to the corner, taking the last bite at corner and stopping with the needle down in background fabric. Raise presser foot. Pivot project, lower presser foot, and take an angled stitch. Raise presser foot. Pivot project, lower presser foot and stitch adjacent side.

10. When stitching outside curves (**Fig. 25**), stop with needle down in background fabric. Raise presser foot and pivot project as needed. Lower presser foot and continue stitching, pivoting as often as necessary to follow curve. Small circles may require pivoting between each stitch.

11. When stitching inside curves (**Fig. 26**), stop with needle down in background fabric. Raise presser foot and pivot project as needed. Lower presser foot and continue stitching, pivoting as often as necessary to follow curve.

12. When stopping stitching, use a lock stitch to sew 5 or 6 stitches in place or use a needle to pull threads to wrong side of background fabric (**Fig. 27**); knot, then trim ends.

13. Carefully tear away stabilizer, if used.

Fig. 25   **Fig. 26**

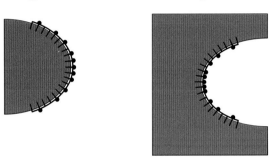

Fig. 22

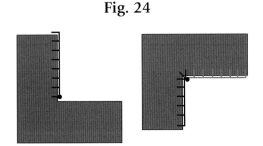

Fig. 23

Fig. 24

Fig. 27

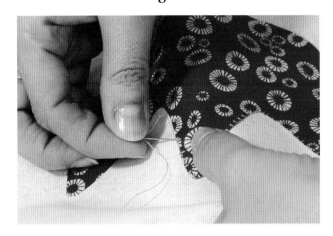

BORDERS
ADDING SQUARED BORDERS

In most cases, our instructions for cutting borders for bed-size quilts include an extra 2" of length at each end for "insurance;" borders will be trimmed after measuring completed center section of quilt top.

1. Mark the center of each edge of quilt top.
2. Squared borders are usually added to sides, then top and bottom edges of the quilt top center. To add side borders, lay quilt top center on a flat surface; measure across quilt top center to determine length of borders (**Fig. 28**). Trim side borders to the determined length.
3. Mark center of 1 long edge of side border. Matching center marks and raw edges, pin border to quilt top, easing in any fullness; stitch. Press seam allowances toward the border.
4. Measure across center of quilt top, including attached borders, to determine length of top and bottom borders (**Fig. 29**). Trim top/bottom borders to the determined length. Repeat Step 3 to add borders to quilt top.

ADDING MITERED BORDERS

1. Mark the center of each edge of quilt top.
2. Mark center of 1 long edge of top border. Measure across center of quilt top (see **Fig. 28**). Matching center marks and raw edges, pin border to center of quilt top edge. From center of border, measure out ¹/₂ the width of the quilt top in both directions and mark. Match marks on border with corners of quilt top and pin. Easing in any fullness, pin border to quilt top between center and corners. Sew border to quilt top, beginning and ending seams exactly ¹/₄" from each corner of quilt top and backstitching at beginning and end of stitching (**Fig. 30**).
3. Repeat Step 2 to sew bottom, then side borders, to center section of quilt top. To temporarily move first 2 borders out of the way, fold and pin ends as shown in **Fig. 31**.
4. Fold 1 corner of quilt top diagonally with right sides together; use rotary cutting ruler to mark stitching line as shown in **Fig. 32**. Pin strips together along drawn line. Sew on drawn line, backstitching at beginning and end of stitching (**Fig. 33**).

Fig. 28   **Fig. 29**

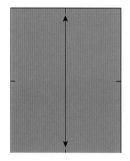 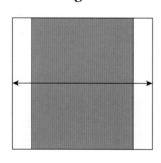

Fig. 31

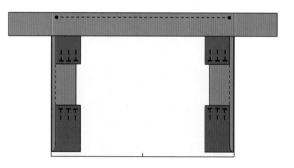

Fig. 30

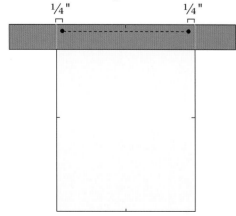

¹/₄"   ¹/₄"

Fig. 32

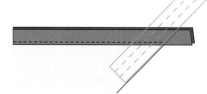

Fig. 33

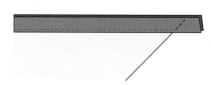

5. Turn mitered corner right side up. Check to see that there is not a gap at the inner end of the seam and that corner does not pucker.
6. Trim seam allowances to $1/4$"; press to 1 side.
7. Repeat Steps 4-6 to miter each remaining corner.

QUILTING

Quilting holds the three layers (top, batting, and backing) of the quilt together and can be done by hand or machine. Because marking, layering, and quilting are interrelated and may be done in different orders depending on circumstances, please read entire **Quilting** *section, pages 89 – 91, before beginning project.*

TYPES OF QUILTING DESIGNS

In the Ditch Quilting
Quilting along seamlines or along edges of appliquéd pieces is called "in the ditch" quilting. This type of quilting should be done on side **opposite** seam allowance and does not have to be marked.

Outline Quilting
Quilting a consistent distance, usually $1/4$", from seam or appliqué is called "outline" quilting. Outline quilting may be marked, or $1/4$" wide masking tape may be placed along seamlines for quilting guide. (Do not leave tape on quilt longer than necessary, since it may leave an adhesive residue.)

Motif Quilting
Quilting a design, such as a feathered wreath, is called "motif" quilting. This type of quilting should be marked before basting quilt layers together.

Echo Quilting
Quilting that follows the outline of an appliquéd or pieced design with two or more parallel lines is called "echo" quilting. This type of quilting does not need to be marked.

Channel Quilting
Quilting with straight, parallel lines is called "channel" quilting. This type of quilting may be marked or stitched using a guide.

Crosshatch Quilting
Quilting straight lines in a grid pattern is called "crosshatch" quilting. Lines may be stitched parallel to edges of quilt or stitched diagonally. This type of quilting may be marked or stitched using a guide.

Meandering Quilting
Quilting in random curved lines and swirls is called "meandering" quilting. Quilting lines should not cross or touch each other. This type of quilting does not need to be marked.

Stipple Quilting
Meandering quilting that is very closely spaced is called "stipple" quilting. Stippling will flatten the area quilted and is often stitched in background areas to raise appliquéd or pieced designs. This type of quilting does not need to be marked.

MARKING QUILTING LINES
Quilting lines may be marked using fabric marking pencils, chalk markers, water- or air-soluble pens.

Simple quilting designs may be marked with chalk or chalk pencil after basting. A small area may be marked, then quilted, before moving to next area to be marked. Intricate designs should be marked before basting using a more durable marker.

Caution: Pressing may permanently set some marks. **Test** different markers **on scrap fabric** to find one that marks clearly and can be thoroughly removed.

A wide variety of pre-cut quilting stencils, as well as entire books of quilting patterns, are available. Using a stencil makes it easier to mark intricate or repetitive designs.

To make a stencil from a pattern, center template plastic over pattern and use a permanent marker to trace pattern onto plastic. Use a craft knife with single or double blade to cut channels along traced lines (**Fig. 34**).

PREPARING THE BACKING

To allow for slight shifting of quilt top during quilting, backing should be approximately 4" larger on all sides. Yardage requirements listed for quilt backings are calculated for 43"/44"w fabric. Using 90"w or 108"w fabric for the backing of a bed-sized quilt may eliminate piecing. To piece a backing using 43"/44"w fabric, use the following instructions.

1. Measure length and width of quilt top; add 8" to each measurement.
2. If determined width is 79" or less, cut backing fabric into two lengths slightly longer than determined *length* measurement. Trim selvages. Place lengths with right sides facing and sew long edges together, forming tube (**Fig. 35**). Match seams and press along one fold (**Fig. 36**). Cut along pressed fold to form single piece (**Fig. 37**).
3. If determined width is more than 79", it may require less fabric yardage if the backing is pieced horizontally. Divide determined *length* measurement by 40" to determine how many widths will be needed. Cut required number of widths the determined *width* measurement. Trim selvages. Sew long edges together to form single piece.
4. Trim backing to size determined in Step 1; press seam allowances open.

CHOOSING THE BATTING

The appropriate batting will make quilting easier. For fine hand quilting, choose low-loft batting. All cotton or cotton/polyester blend battings work well for machine quilting because the cotton helps "grip" quilt layers. If quilt is to be tied, a high-loft batting, sometimes called extra-loft or fat batting, may be used to make quilt "fluffy."

Types of batting include cotton, polyester, wool, cotton/polyester blend, cotton/wool blend, and silk.

When selecting batting, refer to package labels for characteristics and care instructions. Cut batting same size as prepared backing.

Fig. 34

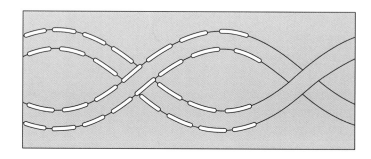

Fig. 35   **Fig. 36**   **Fig. 37**

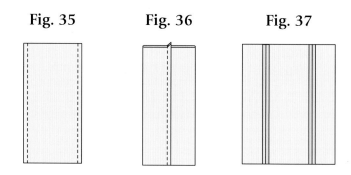

ASSEMBLING THE QUILT

1. Examine wrong side of quilt top closely; trim any seam allowances and clip any threads that may show through front of the quilt. Press quilt top, being careful not to "set" any marked quilting lines.

2. Place backing *wrong* side up on flat surface. Use masking tape to tape edges of backing to surface. Place batting on top of backing fabric. Smooth batting gently, being careful not to stretch or tear. Center quilt top *right* side up on batting.

3. If machine quilting, use 1" rustproof safety pins to "pin-baste" all layers together, spacing pins approximately 4" apart. Begin at center and work toward outer edges to secure all layers. If possible, place pins away from areas that will be quilted, although pins may be removed as needed when quilting.

MACHINE QUILTING METHODS

Use general-purpose thread in bobbin. Do not use quilting thread. Thread the needle of machine with general-purpose thread or transparent monofilament thread to make quilting blend with quilt top fabrics. Use decorative thread, such as a metallic or contrasting-color general-purpose thread, to make quilting lines stand out more.

Straight-Line Quilting

The term "straight-line" is somewhat deceptive, since curves (especially gentle ones) as well as straight lines can be stitched with this technique.

1. Set stitch length for six to ten stitches per inch and attach walking foot to sewing machine.

2. Determine which section of quilt will have longest continuous quilting line, oftentimes area from center top to center bottom. Roll up and secure each edge of quilt to help reduce the bulk, keeping fabrics smooth. Smaller projects may not need to be rolled.

3. Begin stitching on longest quilting line, using very short stitches for the first $1/4$" to "lock" quilting. Stitch across project, using one hand on each side of walking foot to slightly spread fabric and to guide fabric through machine. Lock stitches at end of quilting line.

4. Continue machine quilting, stitching longer quilting lines first to stabilize quilt before moving on to other areas.

Free-Motion Quilting

Free-motion quilting may be free form or may follow a marked pattern.

1. Attach darning foot to sewing machine and lower or cover feed dogs.

2. Position quilt under darning foot; lower foot. Holding top thread, take a stitch and pull bobbin thread to top of quilt. To "lock" beginning of quilting line, hold top and bobbin threads while making three to five stitches in place.

3. Use one hand on each side of darning foot to slightly spread fabric and to move fabric through the machine. Even stitch length is achieved by using smooth, flowing hand motion and steady machine speed. Slow machine speed and fast hand movement will create long stitches. Fast machine speed and slow hand movement will create short stitches. Move quilt sideways, back and forth, in a circular motion, or in a random motion to create desired designs; do not rotate quilt. Lock stitches at end of each quilting line.

MAKING A HANGING SLEEVE

Attaching a hanging sleeve to back of wall hanging or quilt before the binding is added allows project to be displayed on wall.

1. Measure width of quilt top edge and subtract 1". Cut piece of fabric 7"w by determined measurement.

2. Press short edges of fabric piece $1/4$" to wrong side; press edges $1/4$" to wrong side again and machine stitch in place.

3. Matching wrong sides, fold piece in half lengthwise to form tube.

4. Follow project instructions to sew binding to quilt top and to trim backing and batting. Before Blindstitching binding to backing, match raw edges and stitch hanging sleeve to center top edge on back of quilt.

5. Finish binding quilt, treating hanging sleeve as part of backing.

6. Blindstitch bottom of hanging sleeve to backing, taking care not to stitch through to front of quilt.

7. Insert dowel or slat into hanging sleeve.

MAKING A CONTINUOUS BIAS STRIP

Bias strips for binding or appliqué can simply be cut and pieced to desired length. However, when a long length of binding is needed, the "continuous" method is quick and accurate.

1. Use square cut from binding fabric called for in project instructions. Cut square in half diagonally to make two triangles.
2. With right sides together and using ¹/₄" seam allowance, sew triangles together (**Fig. 38**); press seam allowances open.
3. On wrong side of fabric, draw lines the width of binding as specified in project instructions (**Fig. 39**). Cut off any remaining fabric less than this width.
4. With right sides inside, bring short edges together to form tube; match raw edges so that first drawn line of top section meets second drawn line of bottom section (**Fig. 40**).
5. Carefully pin edges together by inserting pins through drawn lines at point where drawn lines intersect, making sure pins go through intersections on both sides. Using ¹/₄" seam allowance, sew edges together; press seam allowances open.
6. To cut continuous strip, begin cutting along first drawn line (**Fig. 41**). Continue cutting along drawn line around tube.
7. Trim ends of bias strip square.

Fig. 38

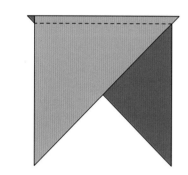

Fig. 39

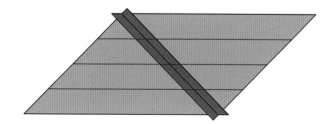

Fig. 40

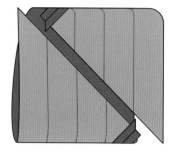

Fig. 41

ATTACHING BINDING WITH MITERED CORNERS

1. Matching wrong sides and raw edges, press continuous strip in half lengthwise to complete binding.
2. Beginning with one end near center on bottom edge of quilt, lay binding around quilt to make sure that seams in binding will not end up at a corner. Adjust placement if necessary. Matching raw edges of binding to raw edge of quilt top, pin binding to right side of quilt along one edge.
3. When you reach first corner, mark $1/4$" from corner of quilt top (**Fig. 42**).

4. Beginning approximately 10" from end of binding and using $1/4$" seam allowance, sew binding to quilt, backstitching at beginning of stitching and at mark (**Fig. 43**). Lift needle out of fabric and clip thread.
5. Fold binding as shown in **Figs. 44 – 45** and pin binding to adjacent side, matching raw edges. When you've reached the next corner, mark $1/4$" from edge of quilt top.
6. Backstitching at edge of quilt top, sew pinned binding to quilt (**Fig. 46**); backstitch at the next mark. Lift needle out of fabric and clip thread.

Fig. 44

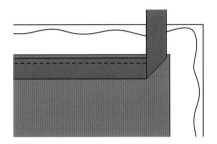

Fig. 45

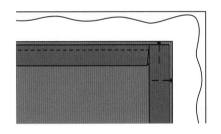

Fig. 46

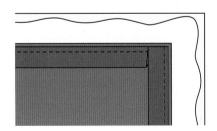

Fig. 42

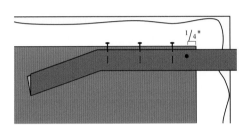

Fig. 43

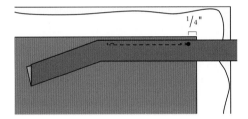

7. Continue sewing binding to quilt, stopping approximately 10" from starting point (**Fig. 47**).

8. Bring beginning and end of binding to center of opening and fold each end back, leaving a ¹/₄" space between folds (**Fig. 48**). Finger press folds.

9. Unfold ends of binding and draw a line across wrong side in finger-pressed crease. Draw a line through the lengthwise pressed fold of binding at the same spot to create a cross mark. With edge of ruler at cross mark, line up 45° angle marking on ruler with one long side of binding. Draw a diagonal line from edge to edge. Repeat on remaining end, making sure that the two diagonal lines are angled the same way (**Fig. 49**).

10. Matching right sides and diagonal lines, pin binding ends together at right angles (**Fig. 50**).

Fig. 47

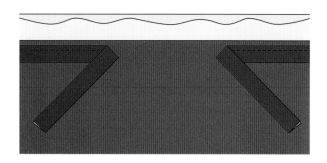

Fig. 48

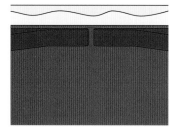

Fig. 49

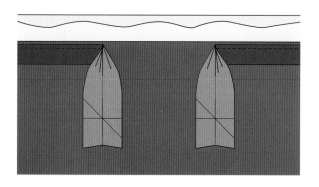

Fig. 50

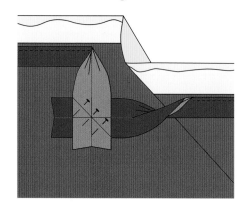

11. Machine stitch along diagonal line (**Fig. 51**), removing pins as you stitch.
12. Lay binding against quilt to double check that it is correct length.
13. Trim binding ends, leaving ¹/₄" seam allowance; press seam open. Stitch binding to quilt.
14. If using 2¹/₂"w binding (finished size ¹/₂"), trim backing and batting a scant ¹/₄" larger than quilt top so that batting and backing will fill the binding when it is folded over to quilt backing. If using narrower binding, trim backing and batting even with edges of quilt top.

15. On one edge of quilt, fold binding over to quilt backing and pin pressed edge in place, covering stitching line (**Fig. 52**). On adjacent side, fold binding over, forming a mitered corner (**Fig. 53**). Repeat to pin remainder of binding in place.
16. Blindstitch binding to backing, taking care not to stitch through to front of quilt.

BLIND STITCH
Come up at 1, go down at 2, and come up at 3 (**Fig. 54**). Length of stitches may be varied as desired.

Fig. 51

Fig. 52   **Fig. 53**

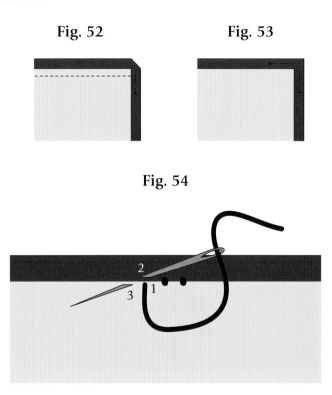

Fig. 54

SIGNING AND DATING YOUR QUILT

A completed quilt is a work of art and should be signed and dated. There are many different ways to do this and numerous books on the subject. The label should reflect the style of the quilt, the occasion or person for which it was made, and the quilter's own particular talents. Following are suggestions for recording the history of quilt or adding a sentiment for future generations.

- Embroider quilter's name, date, and any additional information on quilt top or backing. Matching floss, such as cream floss on white border, will leave a subtle record. Bright or contrasting floss will make the information stand out.

- Make label from muslin and use permanent marker to write information. Use different colored permanent markers to make label more decorative. Stitch label to back of quilt.

- Use photo-transfer paper to add image to white or cream fabric label. Stitch label to back of quilt.

- Piece an extra block from quilt top pattern to use as label. Add information with permanent fabric pen. Appliqué block to back of quilt.

- Write message on appliquéd design from quilt top. Attach appliqué to back of the quilt.

Metric Conversion Chart

Inches x 2.54 = centimeters (cm)	Yards x .9144 = meters (m)
Inches x 25.4 = millimeters (mm)	Yards x 91.44 = centimeters (cm)
Inches x .0254 = meters (m)	Centimeters x .3937 = inches (")
	Meters x 1.0936 = yards (yd)

Standard Equivalents

$\frac{1}{8}$"	3.2 mm	0.32 cm	$\frac{1}{8}$ yard	11.43 cm	0.11 m
$\frac{1}{4}$"	6.35 mm	0.635 cm	$\frac{1}{4}$ yard	22.86 cm	0.23 m
$\frac{3}{8}$"	9.5 mm	0.95 cm	$\frac{3}{8}$ yard	34.29 cm	0.34 m
$\frac{1}{2}$"	12.7 mm	1.27 cm	$\frac{1}{2}$ yard	45.72 cm	0.46 m
$\frac{5}{8}$"	15.9 mm	1.59 cm	$\frac{5}{8}$ yard	57.15 cm	0.57 m
$\frac{3}{4}$"	19.1 mm	1.91 cm	$\frac{3}{4}$ yard	68.58 cm	0.69 m
$\frac{7}{8}$"	22.2 mm	2.22 cm	$\frac{7}{8}$ yard	80 cm	0.8 m
1"	25.4 mm	2.54 cm	1 yard	91.44 cm	0.91 m